"I think a hero is an ordinary individual who finds strength to persevere and endure in spite of overwhelming obstacles."

— Christopher Reeve

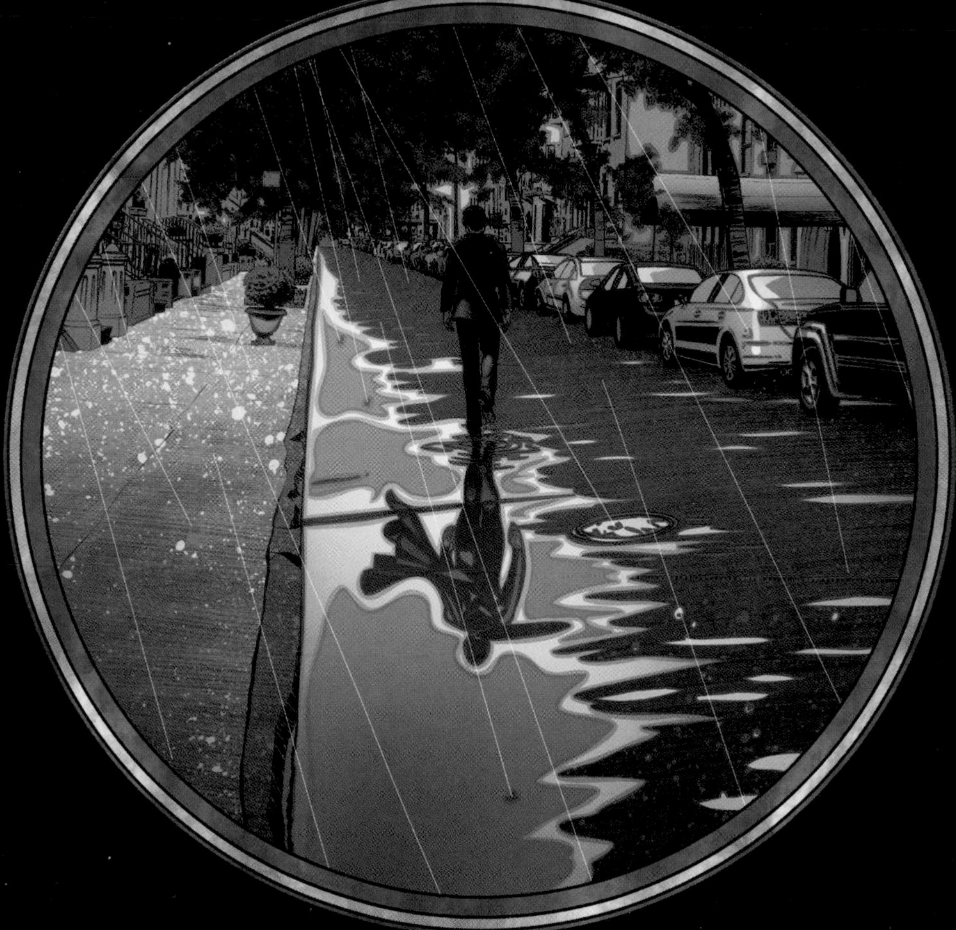

Productivity Ltd Presents

Silicon Heroes

Written By Joseph Floyd
Illustrations by Michael Penick, with colors
By John Rauch
Edited by Mark Irwin

Silicon Heroes. Published by Productivity Ltd, Inc. Office of publication: 1160 Mission St. #510, San Francisco, CA 94103.

Library of Congress Control Number: 2016958264

So It Begins

Entrepreneurs are superheroes. They strive to solve the world's problems. They inspire social change through innovation and improve quality of life with invention. Entrepreneurs perform heroic feats with scarce time, limited resources and against all odds. Yet, most of these heroes toil away in obscurity, hidden away from the media.

Young people grow up idolizing the stars of pop culture and social media, which today are musicians, movie stars and athletes. I want my children to know that there are other heroes in the world - inventors, visionaries, and business leaders. I want my children to look up to these people and to know that they can follow similar paths to success by using their hearts and their brains.

I have been a venture capital investor since 2007 and I have worked with incredible entrepreneurs and investors almost every day since. Starting in 2013, I embarked on my Kauffman Fellows research project to interview CEOs and investors of the most successful startups to determine the character traits most highly correlated with entrepreneurial success.

Silicon Heroes is the product of my research. I specifically chose to weave my learnings into a graphic novel because I wanted readers to let their imaginations power their unique experiences of this classic hero's quest. In the world of Silicon Heroes, some people possess comic book style superpowers. Each power is a metaphor for a specific character trait. Like all superhero sagas, the themes of Silicon Heroes are universal, and it is up to the readers to discover their own meaning.

My goals for Silicon Heroes are to inspire the next generation of entrepreneurs and to share a little of the magic that makes Silicon Valley special. Turn the page to begin your hero's quest.

— Joseph Floyd
December 2016

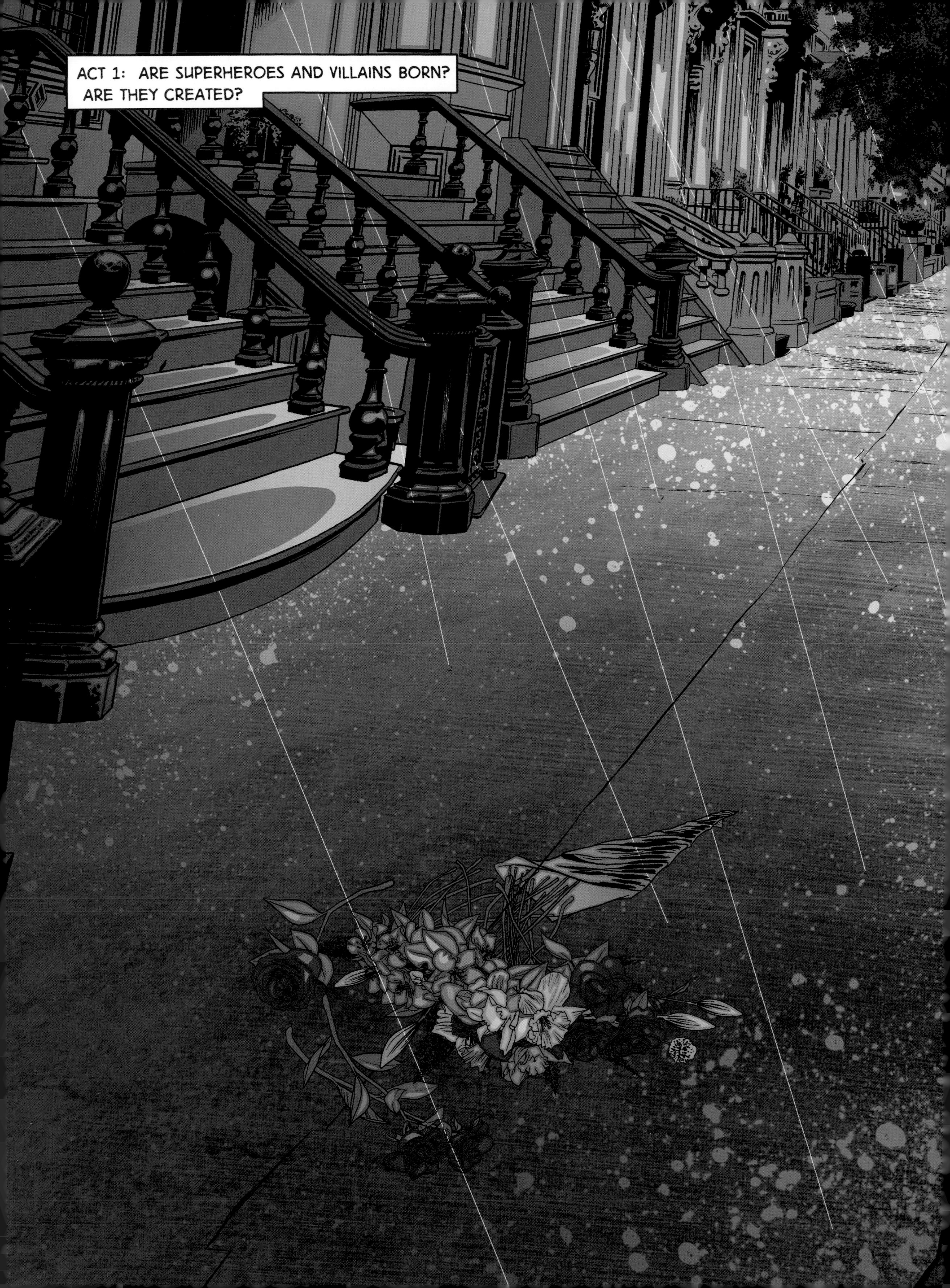
ACT 1: ARE SUPERHEROES AND VILLAINS BORN? ARE THEY CREATED?

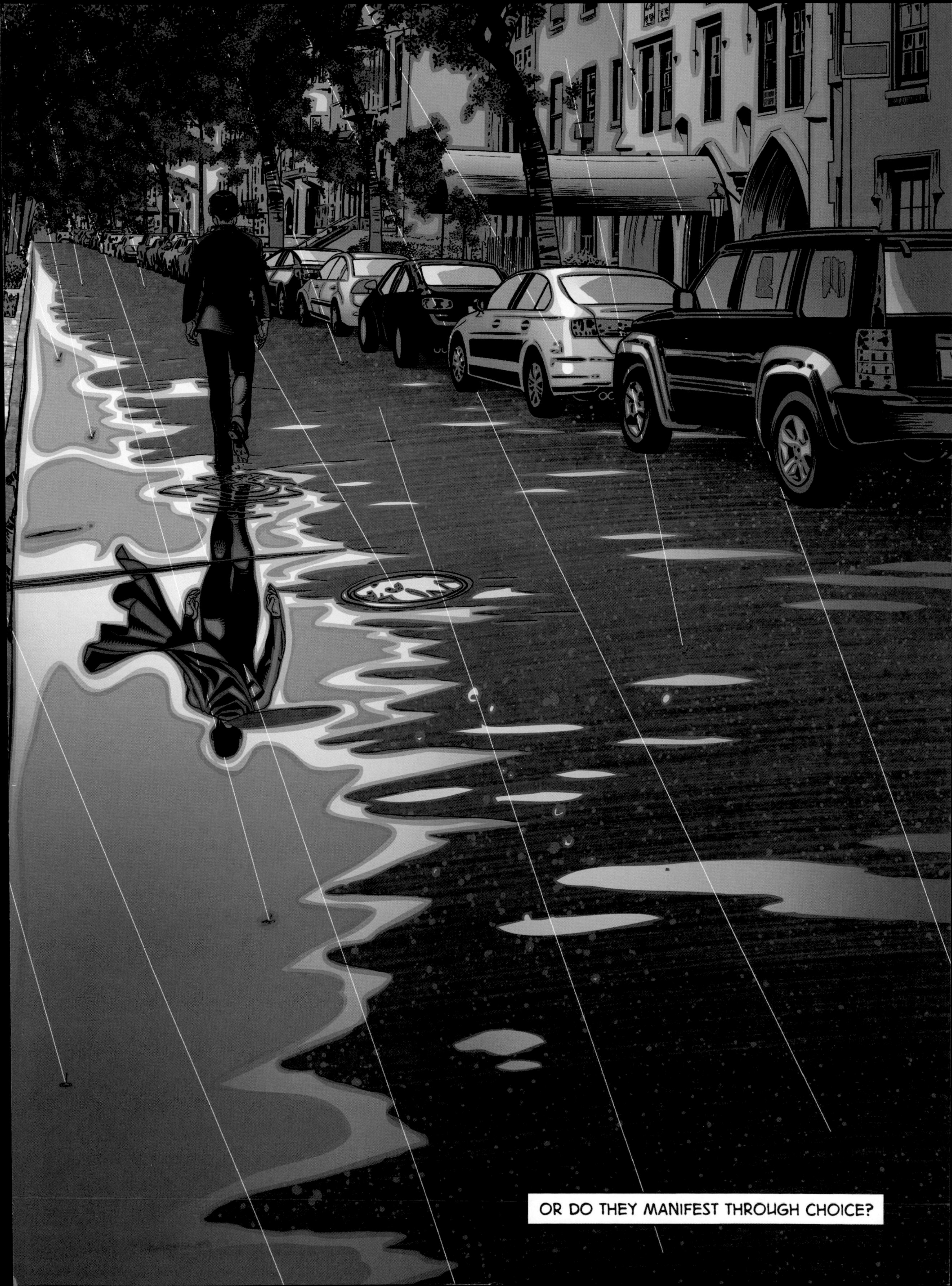
OR DO THEY MANIFEST THROUGH CHOICE?

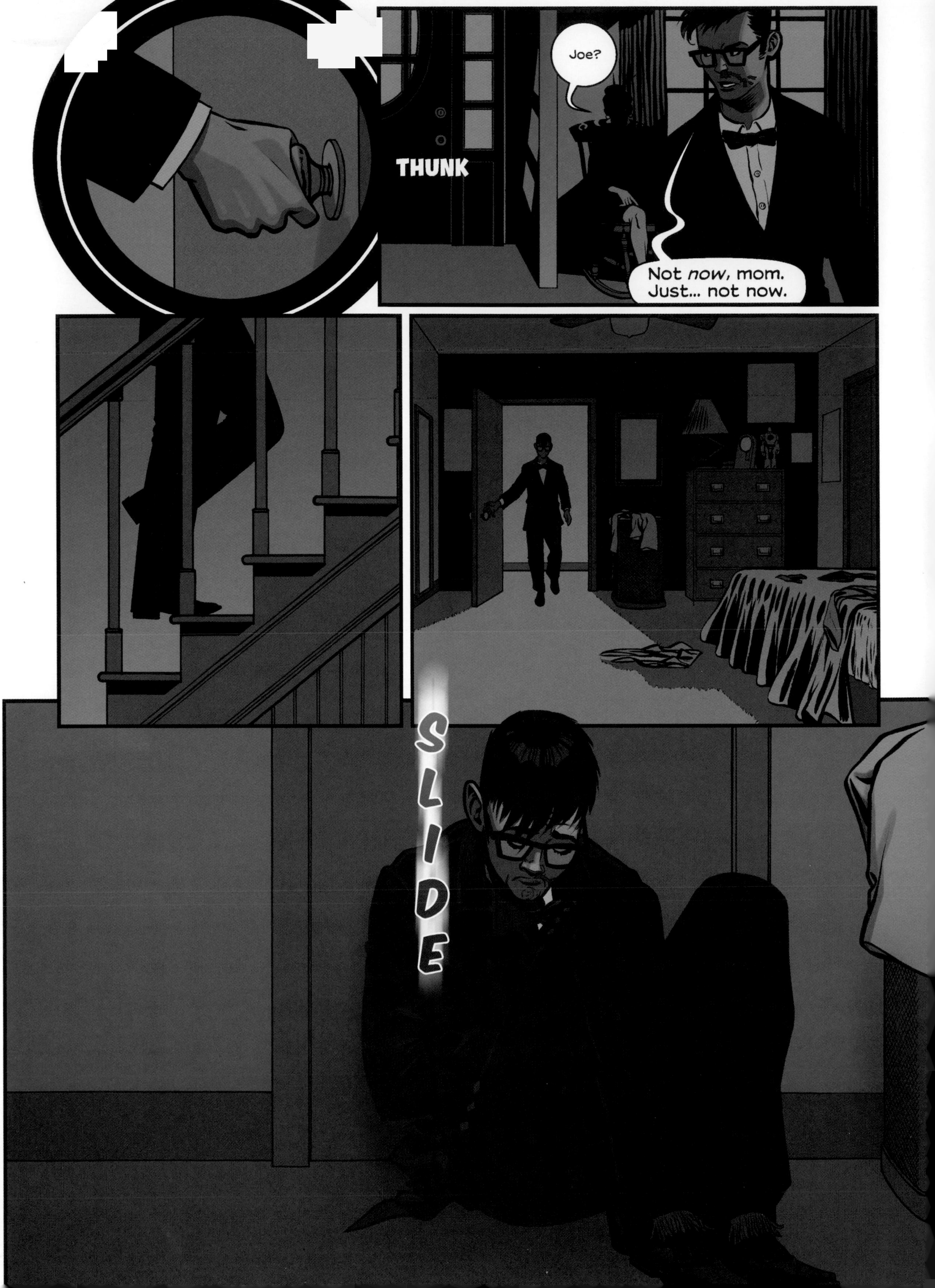
THUNK
Joe?
Not *now*, mom. Just... not now.
SLIDE

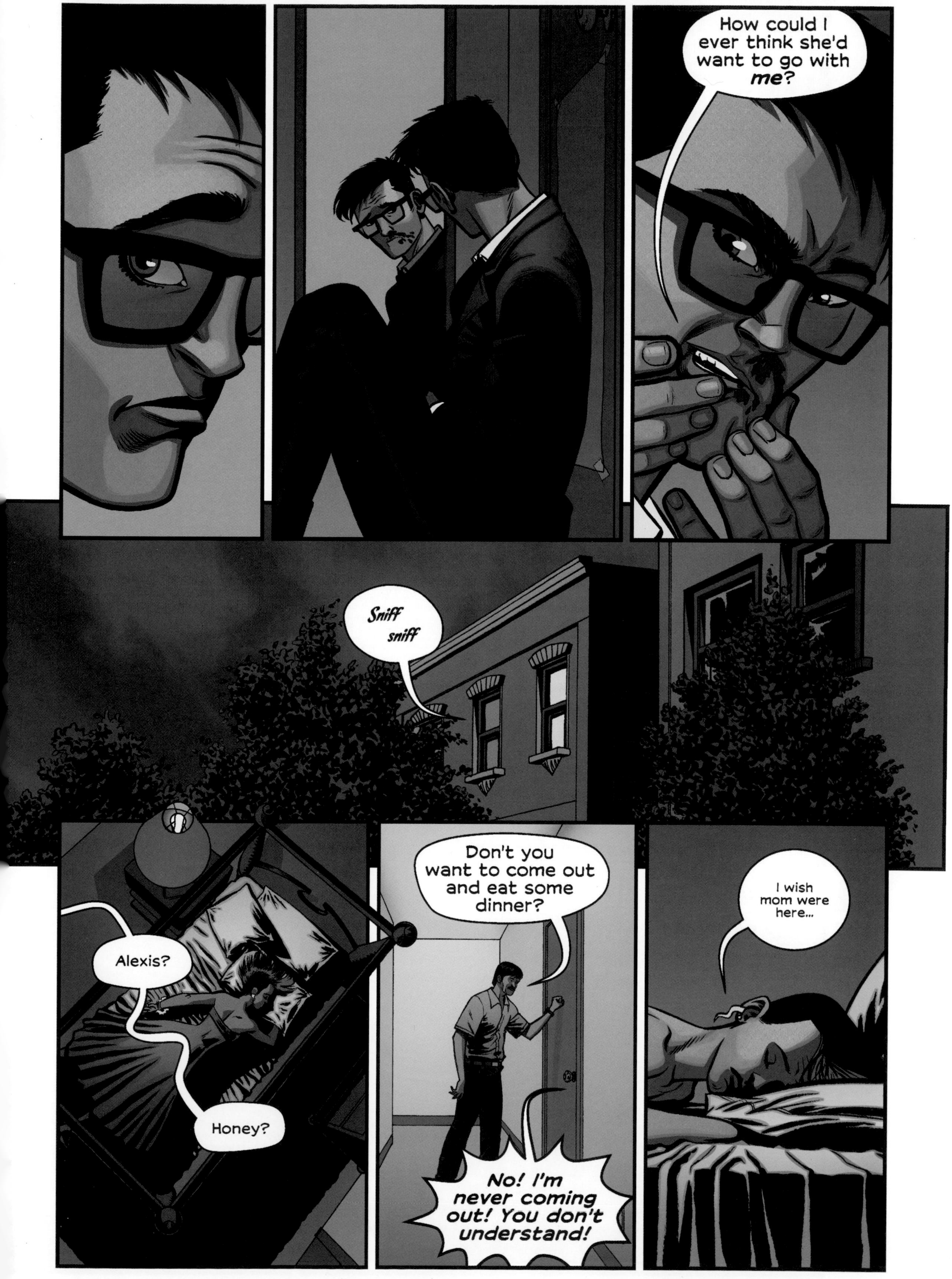
How could I ever think she'd want to go with *me*?
Sniff sniff
Alexis?
Honey?
Don't you want to come out and eat some dinner?
No! I'm never coming out! You don't understand!
I wish mom were here...

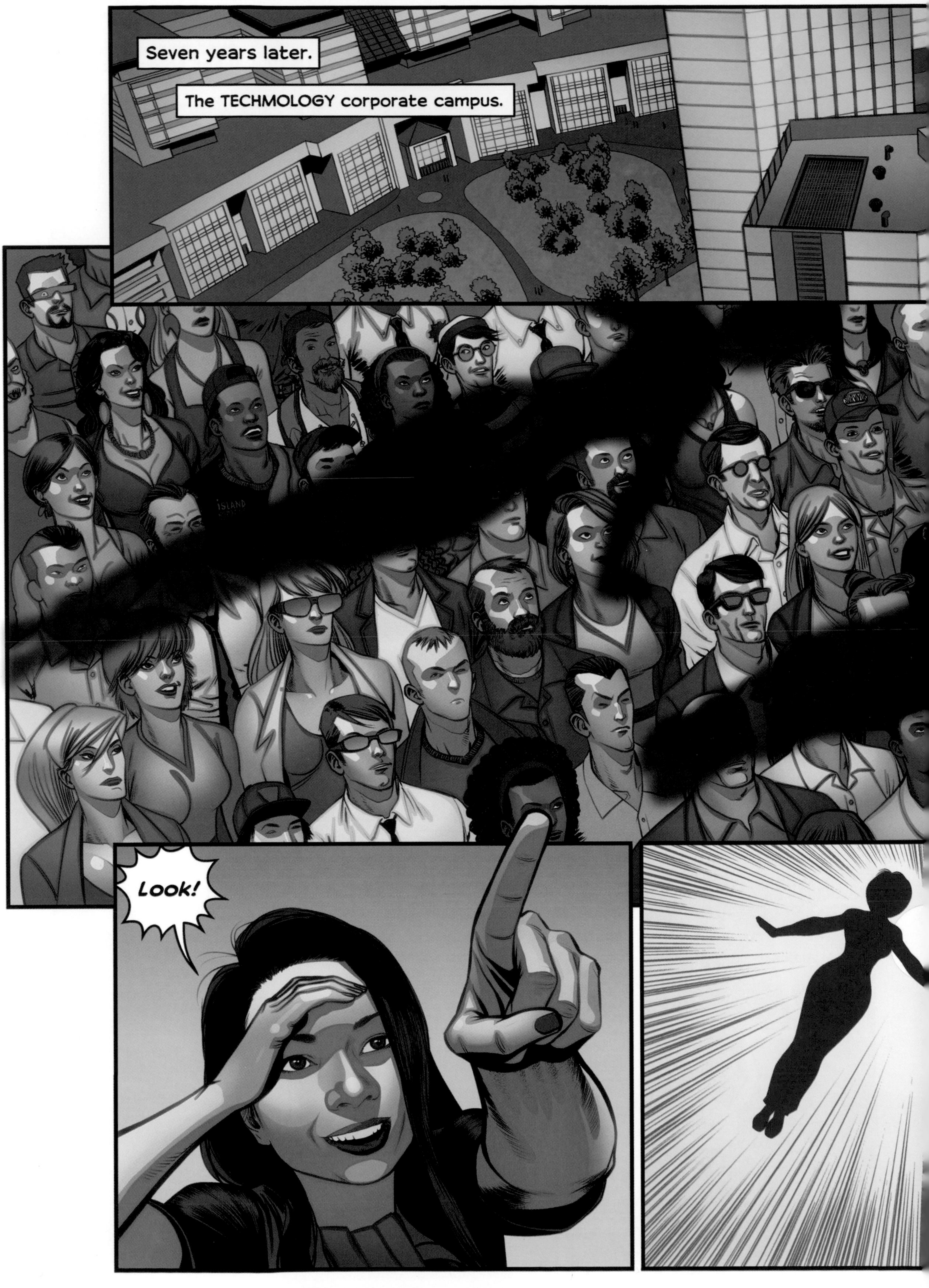
Seven years later.
The TECHMOLOGY corporate campus.
Look!

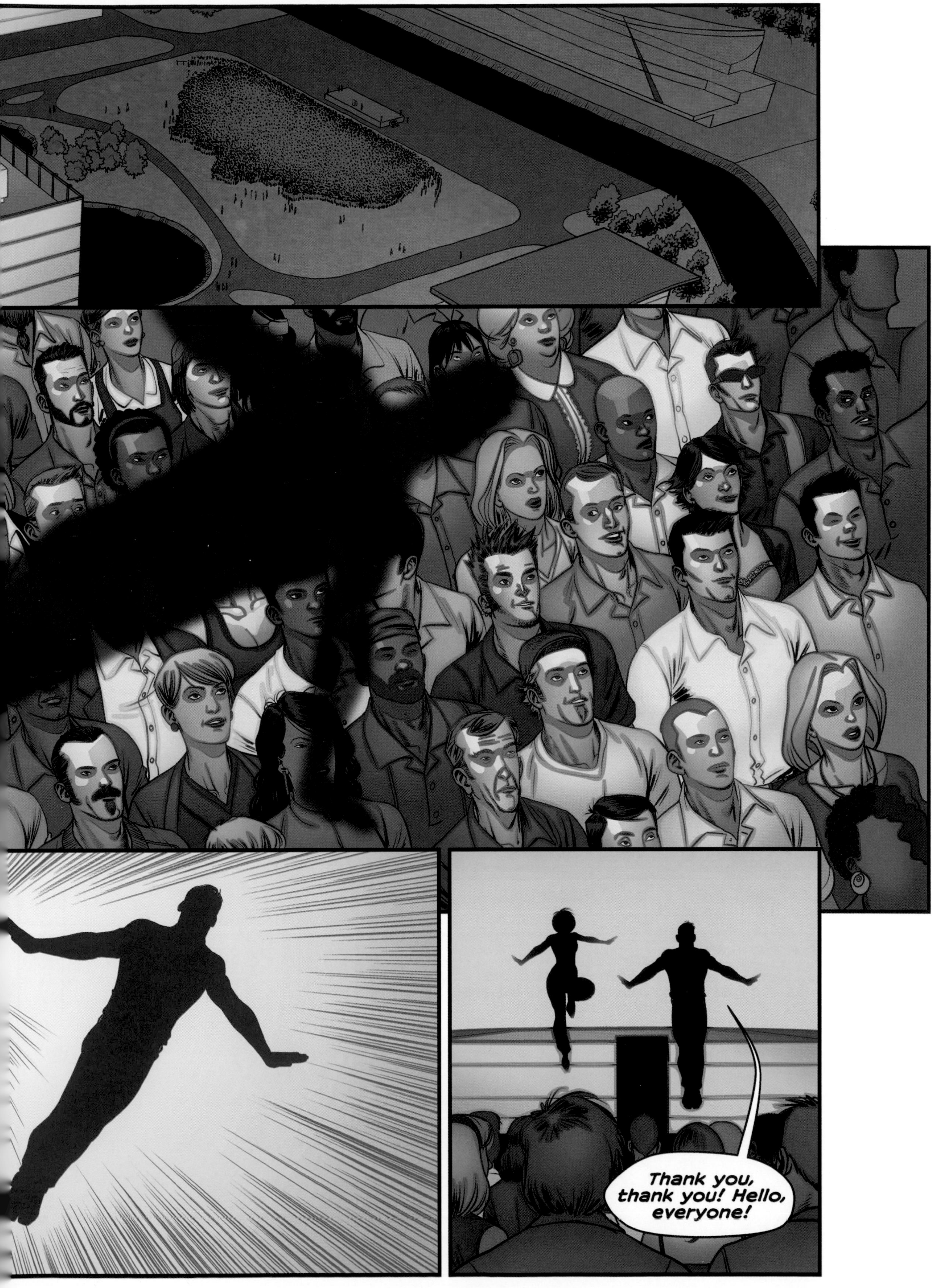
Thank you, thank you! Hello, everyone!

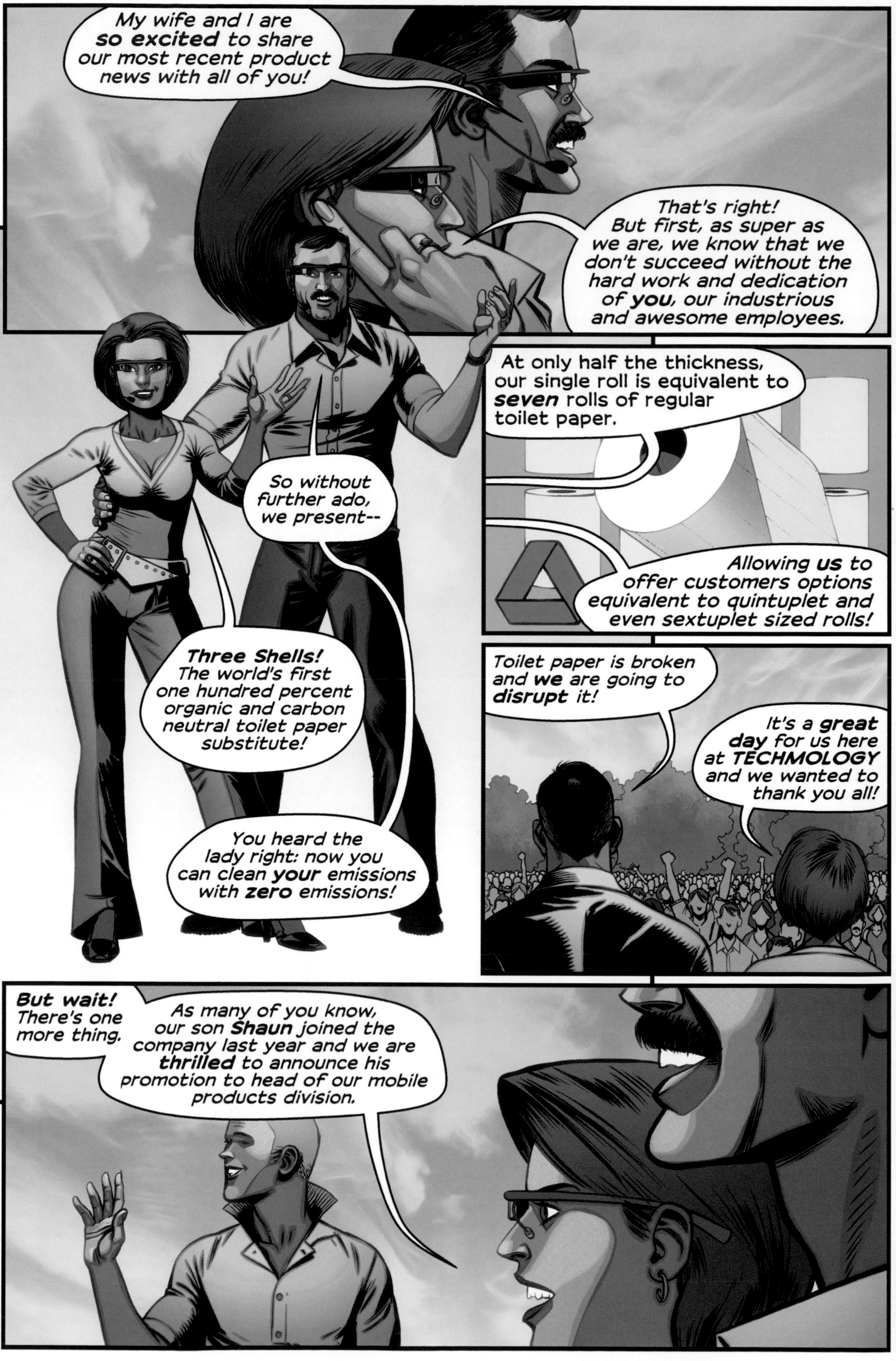
My wife and I are **so excited** to share our most recent product news with all of you!
That's right! But first, as super as we are, we know that we don't succeed without the hard work and dedication of **you**, our industrious and awesome employees.
At only half the thickness, our single roll is equivalent to ***seven*** rolls of regular toilet paper.
Allowing **us** to offer customers options equivalent to quintuplet and even sextuplet sized rolls!
So without further ado, we present--
Three Shells! The world's first one hundred percent organic and carbon neutral toilet paper substitute!
You heard the lady right: now you can clean **your** emissions with **zero** emissions!
Toilet paper is broken and **we** are going to ***disrupt*** it!
It's a **great day** for us here at **TECHMOLOGY** and we wanted to thank you all!
But wait! There's one more thing.
As many of you know, our son **Shaun** joined the company last year and we are **thrilled** to announce his promotion to head of our mobile products division.

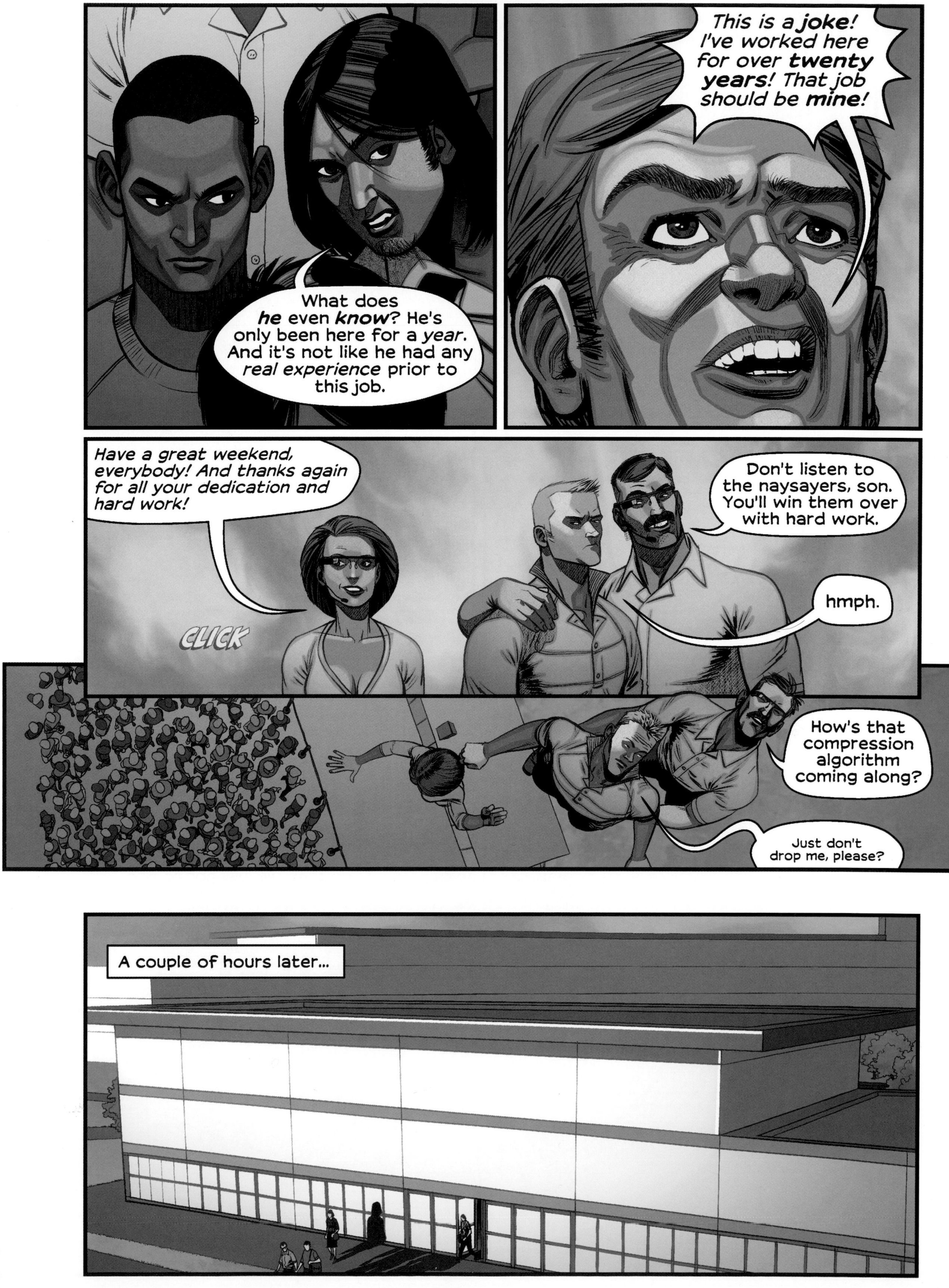
What does he even know? He's only been here for a year. And it's not like he had any real experience prior to this job.
This is a joke! I've worked here for over twenty years! That job should be mine!
Have a great weekend, everybody! And thanks again for all your dedication and hard work!
CLICK
Don't listen to the naysayers, son. You'll win them over with hard work.
hmph.
How's that compression algorithm coming along?
Just don't drop me, please?
A couple of hours later...

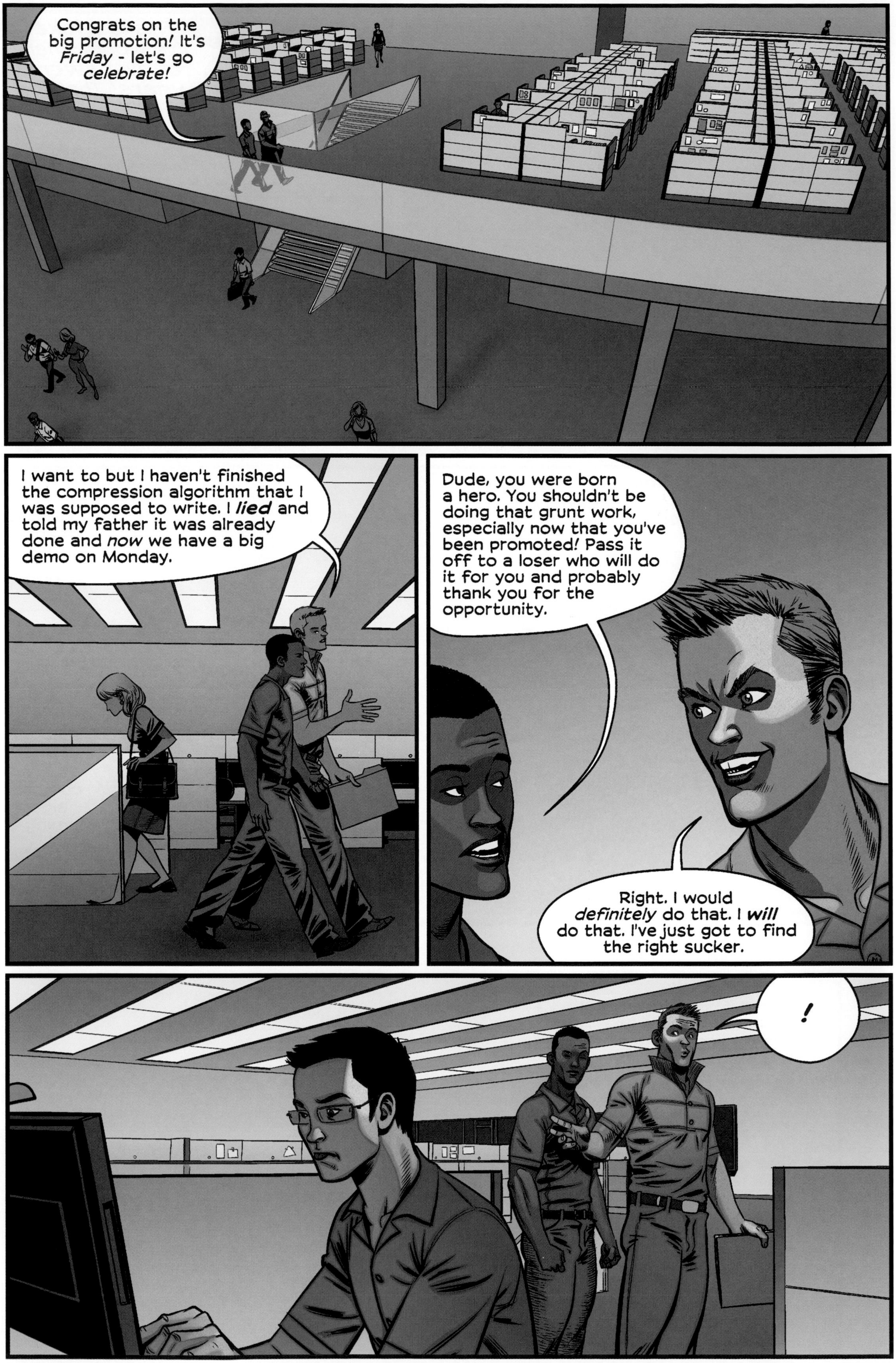
Congrats on the big promotion! It's *Friday* - let's go *celebrate!*
I want to but I haven't finished the compression algorithm that I was supposed to write. I *lied* and told my father it was already done and *now* we have a big demo on Monday.
Dude, you were born a hero. You shouldn't be doing that grunt work, especially now that you've been promoted! Pass it off to a loser who will do it for you and probably thank you for the opportunity.
Right. I would *definitely* do that. I *will* do that. I've just got to find the right sucker.
!

Joe! Buddy! I'm sure you heard about my big promotion. Thanks. I know. Super cool. Anyway, it means I'm too *busy* now to finish the *compression algorithm* I was working on. Which leads me to *you.*

But I thought your *you* to write that.

Nope. He's got me on much more important stuff now, so I'm going to need you to stay late tonight and crank it out for me.

But I'm working on the SoLoMo app right now.

Don't worry about the SoMo-- MoSo-- thethe-- that app. I've got top men working on it.

Who?

Top.

Men.

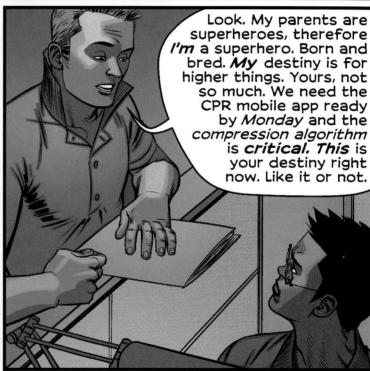

Look. My parents are superheroes, therefore *I'm* a superhero. Born and bred. *My* destiny is for higher things. Yours, not so much. We need the CPR mobile app ready by *Monday* and the *compression algorithm* is *critical. This* is your destiny right now. Like it or not.

Look. Do this, don't *tell* anyone, and I'll make sure you're placed on a *new* team with *superheroes* so you can be cool by association.

Program this code for me and I'll *make sure* you're invited to the fraternity party.

Do my homework for me and *I promise* I'll pick you for my dodgeball team.

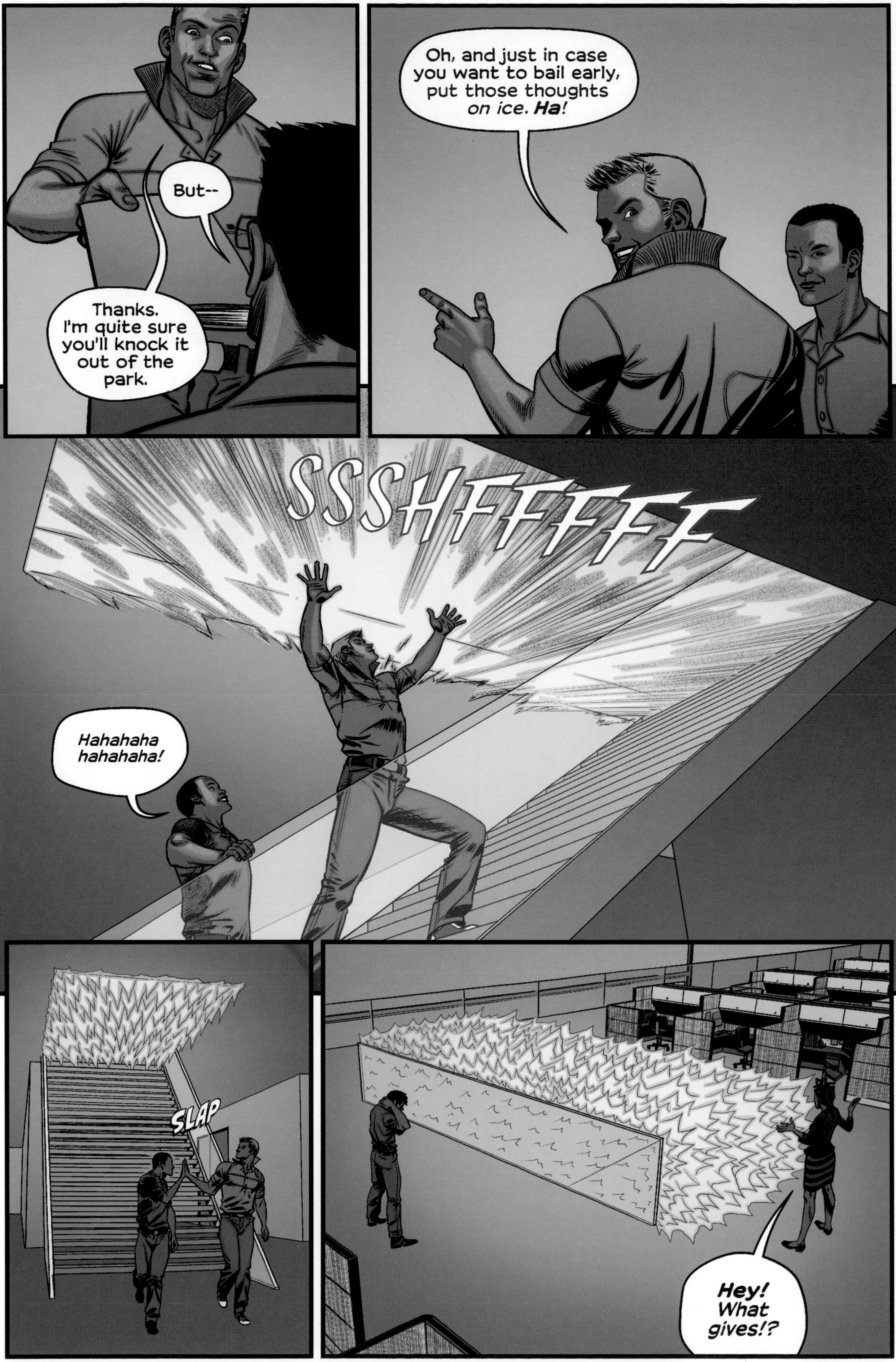
But--
Thanks. I'm quite sure you'll knock it out of the park.
Oh, and just in case you want to bail early, put those thoughts *on ice*. ***Ha***!
SSSHFFFFFF
Hahahaha hahahaha!
SLAP
Hey! What gives!?

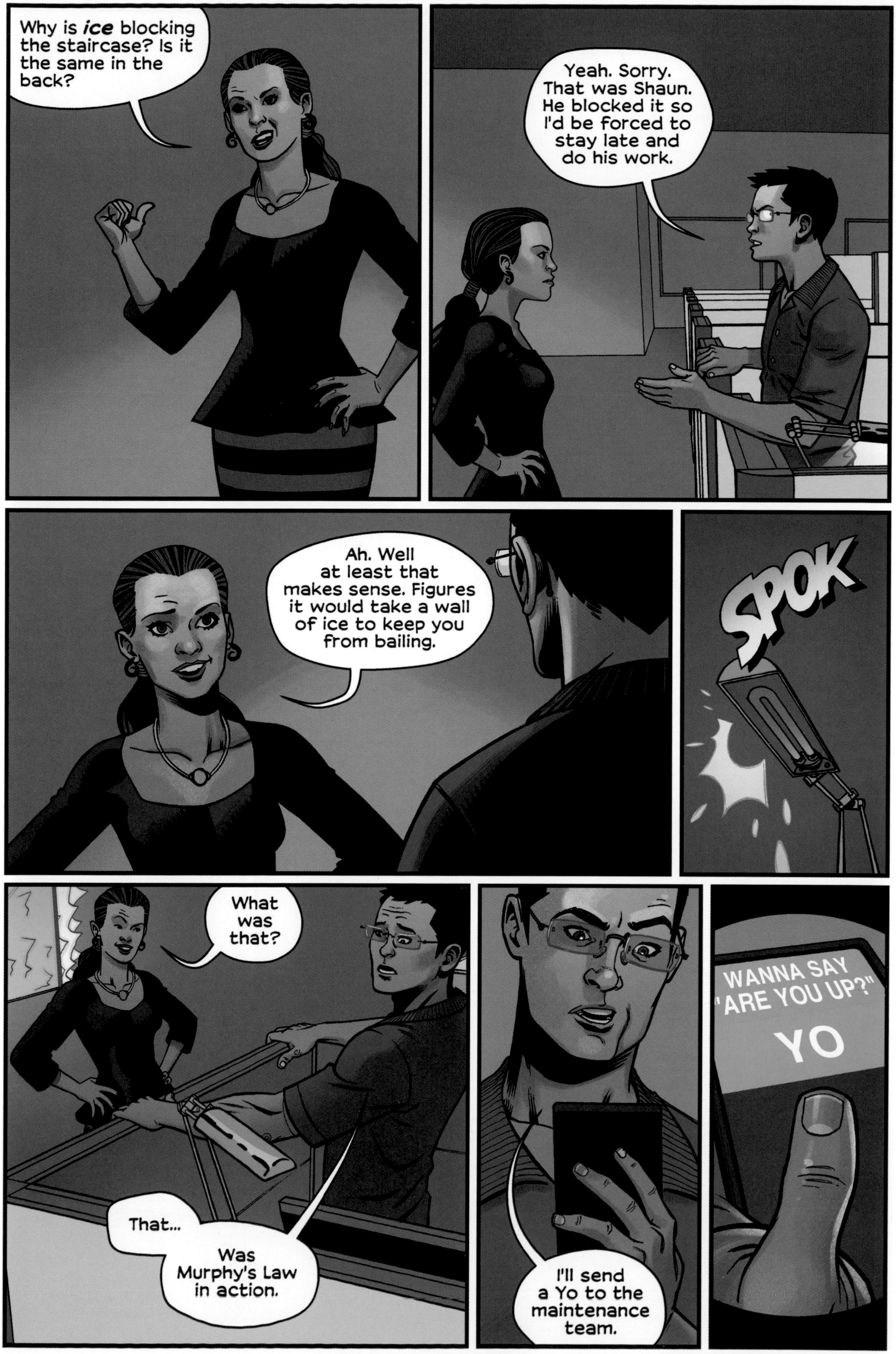
Why is *ice* blocking the staircase? Is it the same in the back?
Yeah. Sorry. That was Shaun. He blocked it so I'd be forced to stay late and do his work.
Ah. Well at least that makes sense. Figures it would take a wall of ice to keep you from bailing.
SPOK
What was that?
That...
Was Murphy's Law in action.
I'll send a Yo to the maintenance team.
WANNA SAY "ARE YOU UP?"
YO

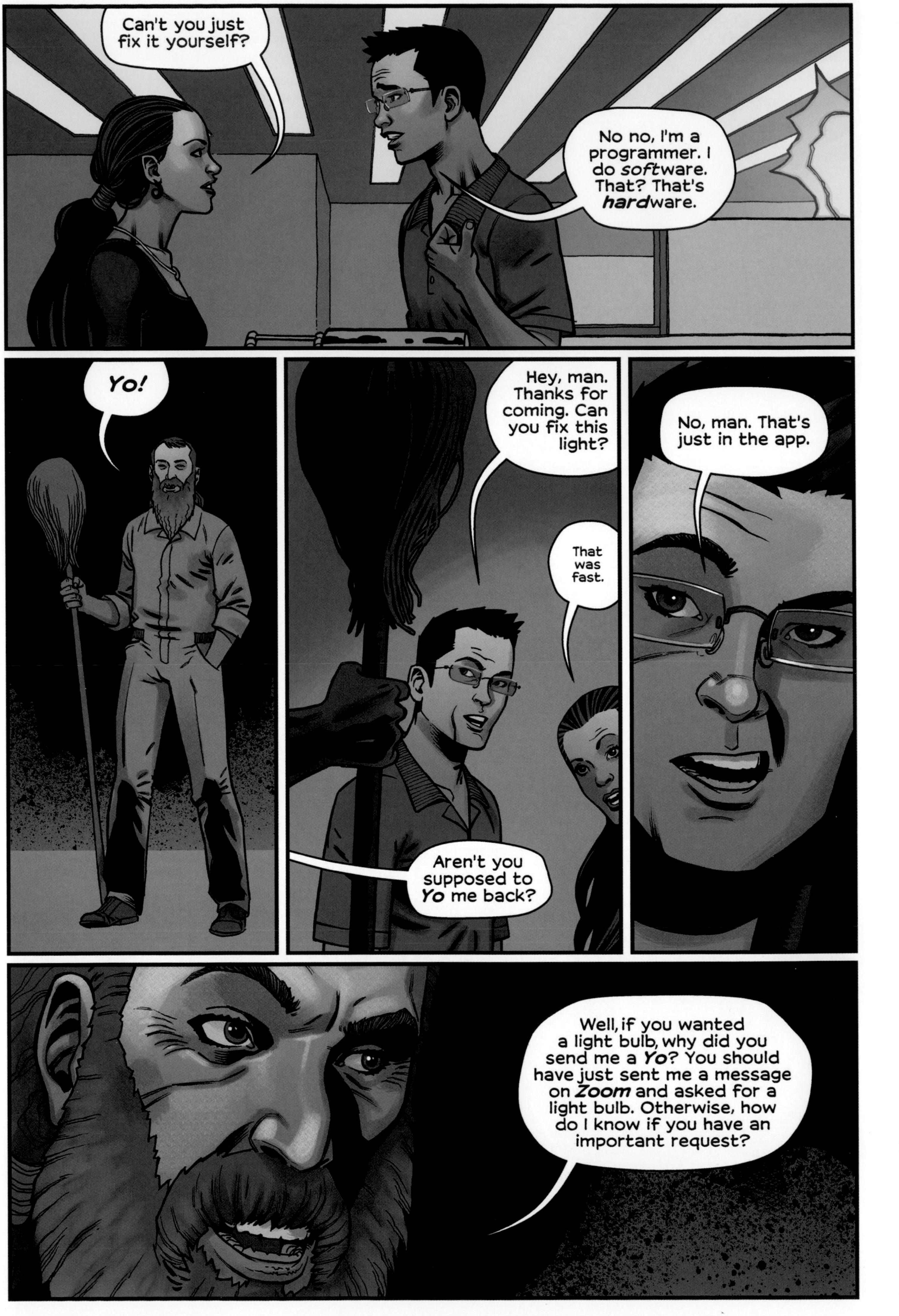
Can't you just fix it yourself?
No no, I'm a programmer. I do *soft*ware. That? That's ***hard***ware.
Yo!
Hey, man. Thanks for coming. Can you fix this light?
That was fast.
Aren't you supposed to *Yo* me back?
No, man. That's just in the app.
Well, if you wanted a light bulb, why did you send me a *Yo*? You should have just sent me a message on *Zoom* and asked for a light bulb. Otherwise, how do I know if you have an important request?

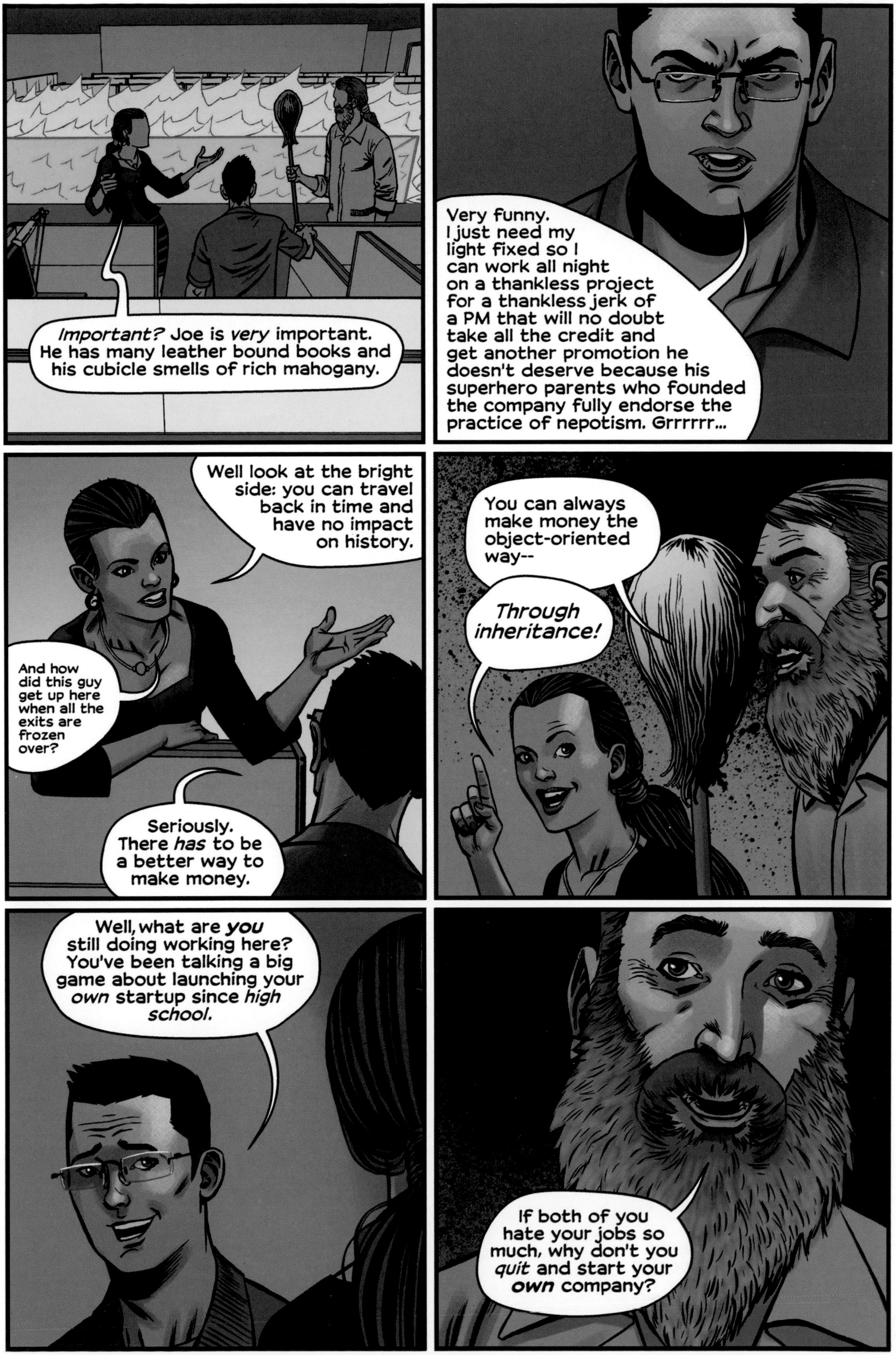
Important? Joe is *very* important. He has many leather bound books and his cubicle smells of rich mahogany.
Very funny. I just need my light fixed so I can work all night on a thankless project for a thankless jerk of a PM that will no doubt take all the credit and get another promotion he doesn't deserve because his superhero parents who founded the company fully endorse the practice of nepotism. Grrrrrr...
Well look at the bright side: you can travel back in time and have no impact on history.
And how did this guy get up here when all the exits are frozen over?
Seriously. There *has* to be a better way to make money.
You can always make money the object-oriented way--
Through inheritance!
Well, what are ***you*** still doing working here? You've been talking a big game about launching your *own* startup since *high school*.
If both of you hate your jobs so much, why don't you *quit* and start your ***own*** company?

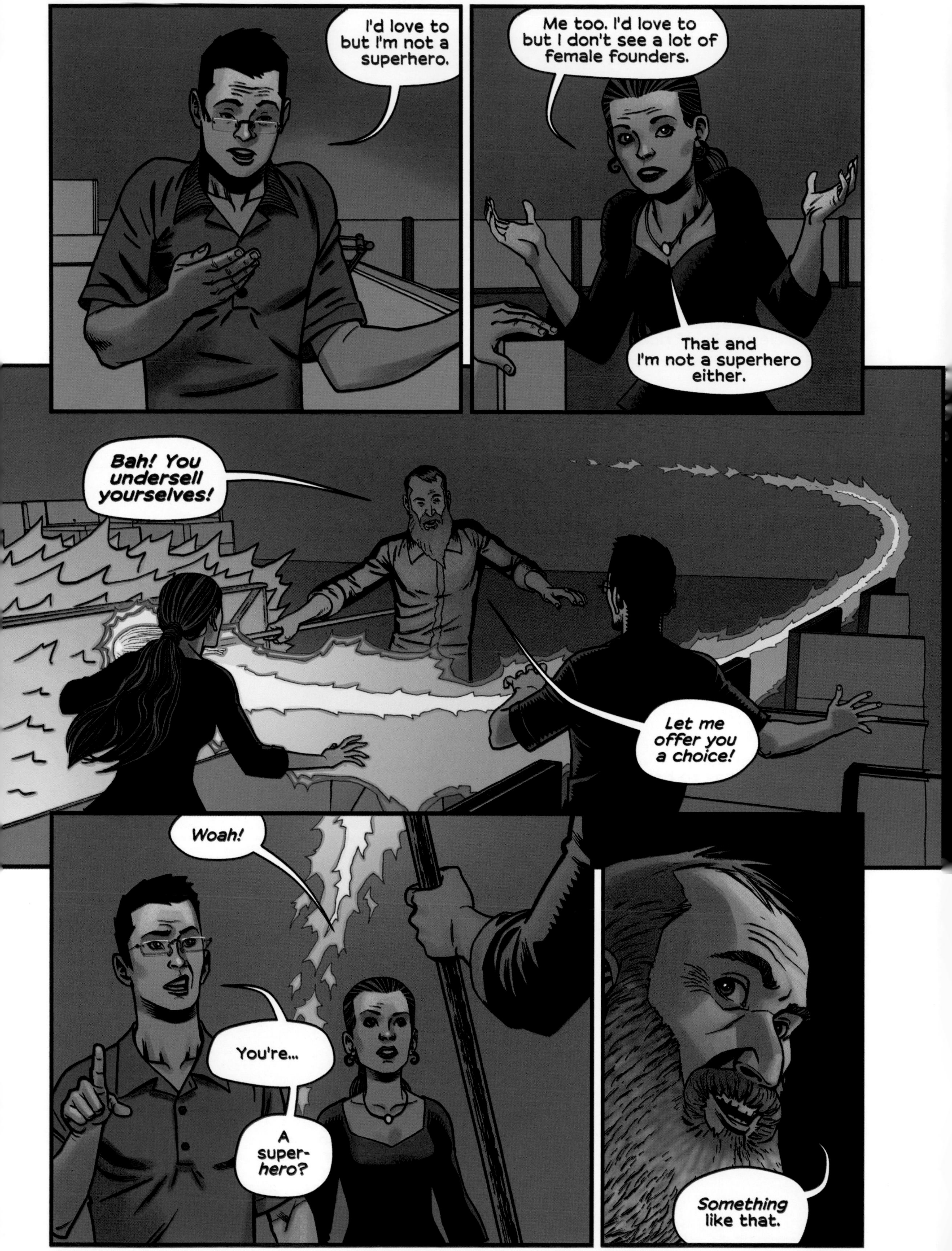
I'd love to but I'm not a superhero.
Me too. I'd love to but I don't see a lot of female founders.
That and I'm not a superhero either.
Bah! You undersell yourselves!
Let me offer you a choice!
Woah!
You're...
A super-hero?
Something like that.

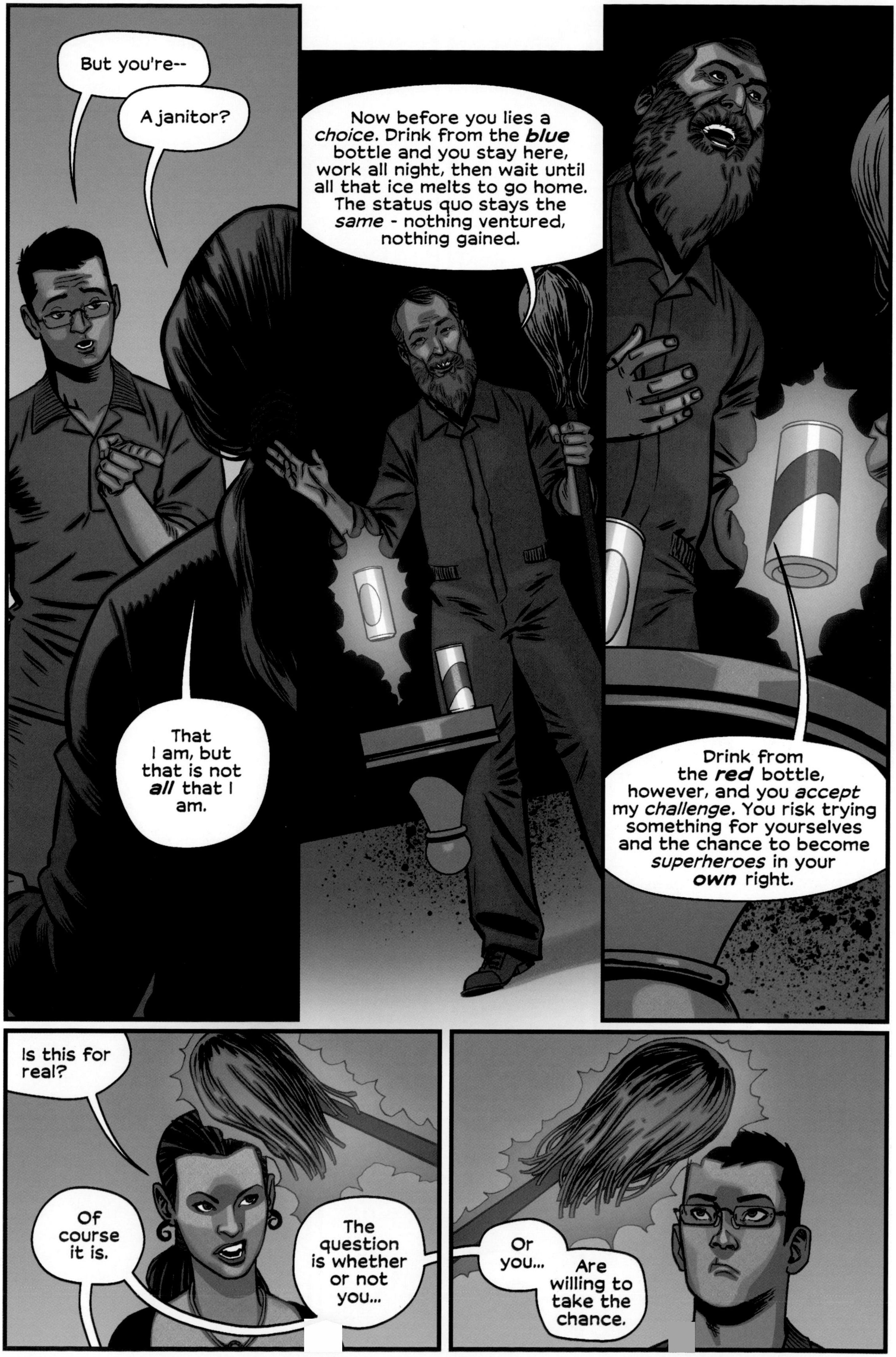

But you're--
A janitor?
That I am, but that is not *all* that I am.
Now before you lies a *choice*. Drink from the ***blue*** bottle and you stay here, work all night, then wait until all that ice melts to go home. The status quo stays the *same* - nothing ventured, nothing gained.
Drink from the ***red*** bottle, however, and you *accept* my *challenge*. You risk trying something for yourselves and the chance to become *superheroes* in your ***own*** right.
Is this for real?
Of course it is.
The question is whether or not you...
Or you...
Are willing to take the chance.

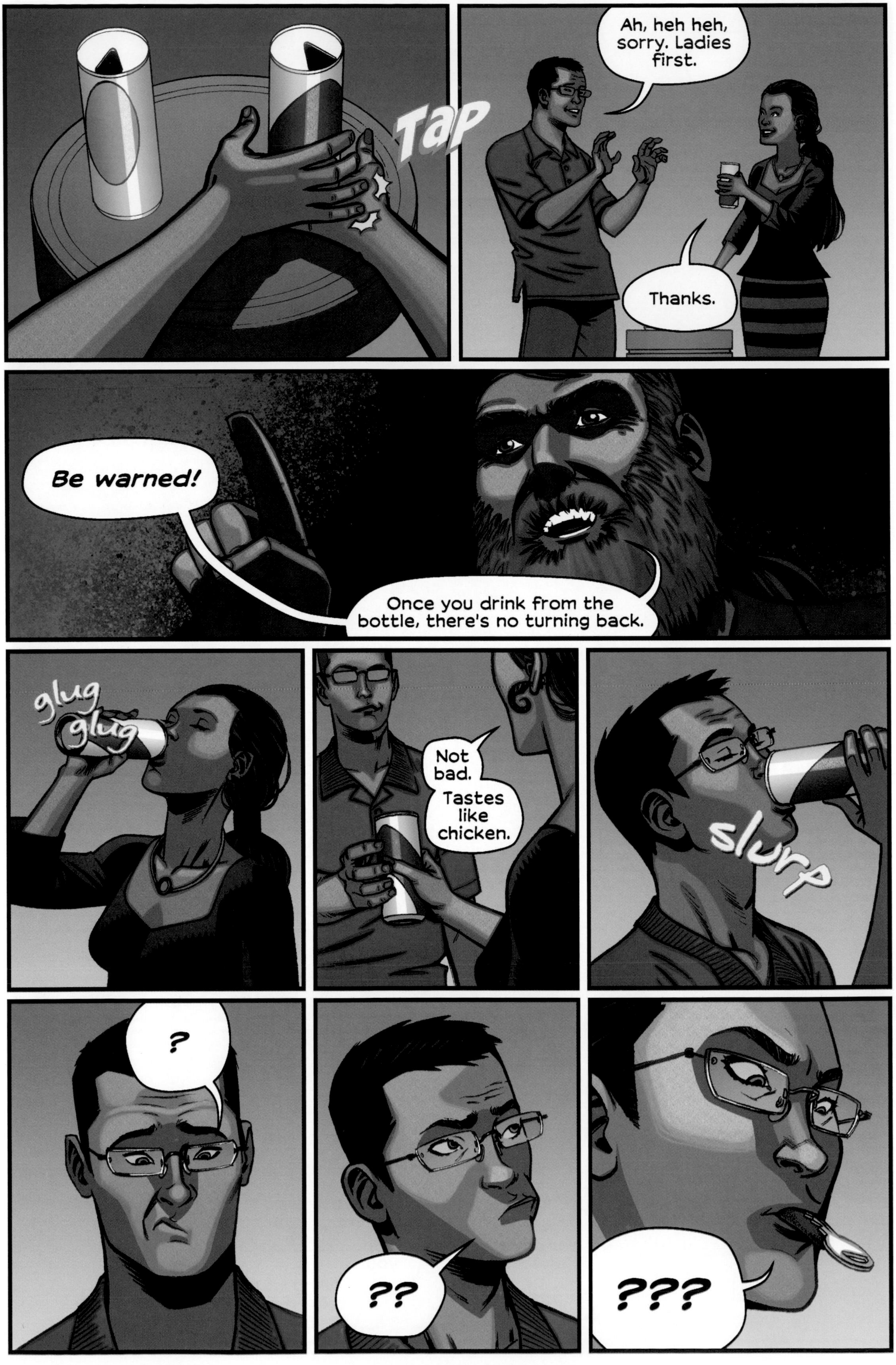
Tap
Ah, heh heh, sorry. Ladies first.
Thanks.
Be warned!
Once you drink from the bottle, there's no turning back.
glug glug
Not bad.
Tastes like chicken.
slurp
?
??
???

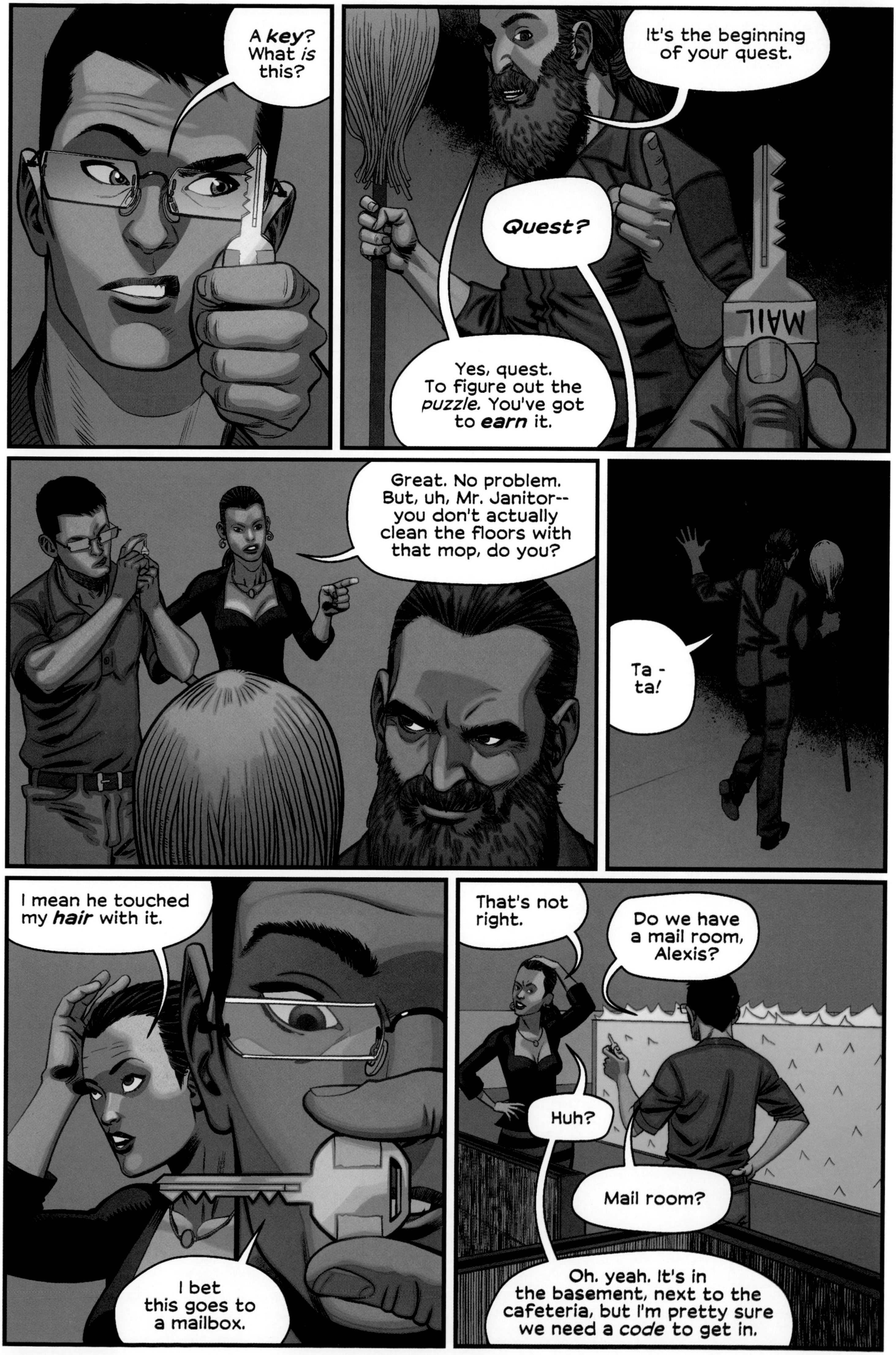
A *key*? What *is* this?
It's the beginning of your quest.
Quest?
Yes, quest. To figure out the *puzzle.* You've got to *earn* it.
MAIL
Great. No problem. But, uh, Mr. Janitor-- you don't actually clean the floors with that mop, do you?
Ta - ta!
I mean he touched my *hair* with it.
I bet this goes to a mailbox.
That's not right.
Do we have a mail room, Alexis?
Huh?
Mail room?
Oh. yeah. It's in the basement, next to the cafeteria, but I'm pretty sure we need a *code* to get in.

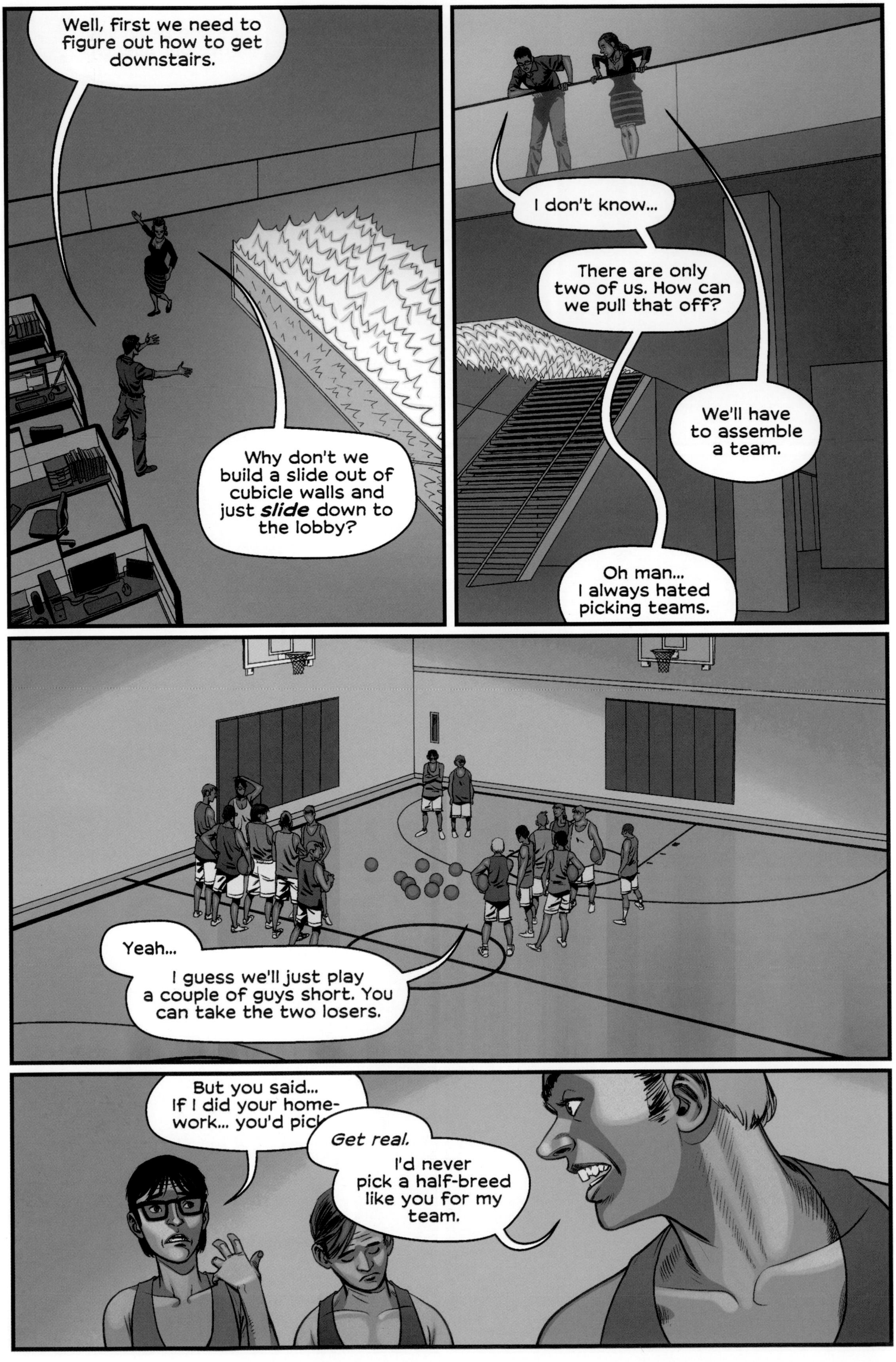
Well, first we need to figure out how to get downstairs.
Why don't we build a slide out of cubicle walls and just *slide* down to the lobby?
I don't know...
There are only two of us. How can we pull that off?
We'll have to assemble a team.
Oh man... I always hated picking teams.
Yeah...
I guess we'll just play a couple of guys short. You can take the two losers.
But you said... If I did your home-work... you'd pick
Get real.
I'd never pick a half-breed like you for my team.

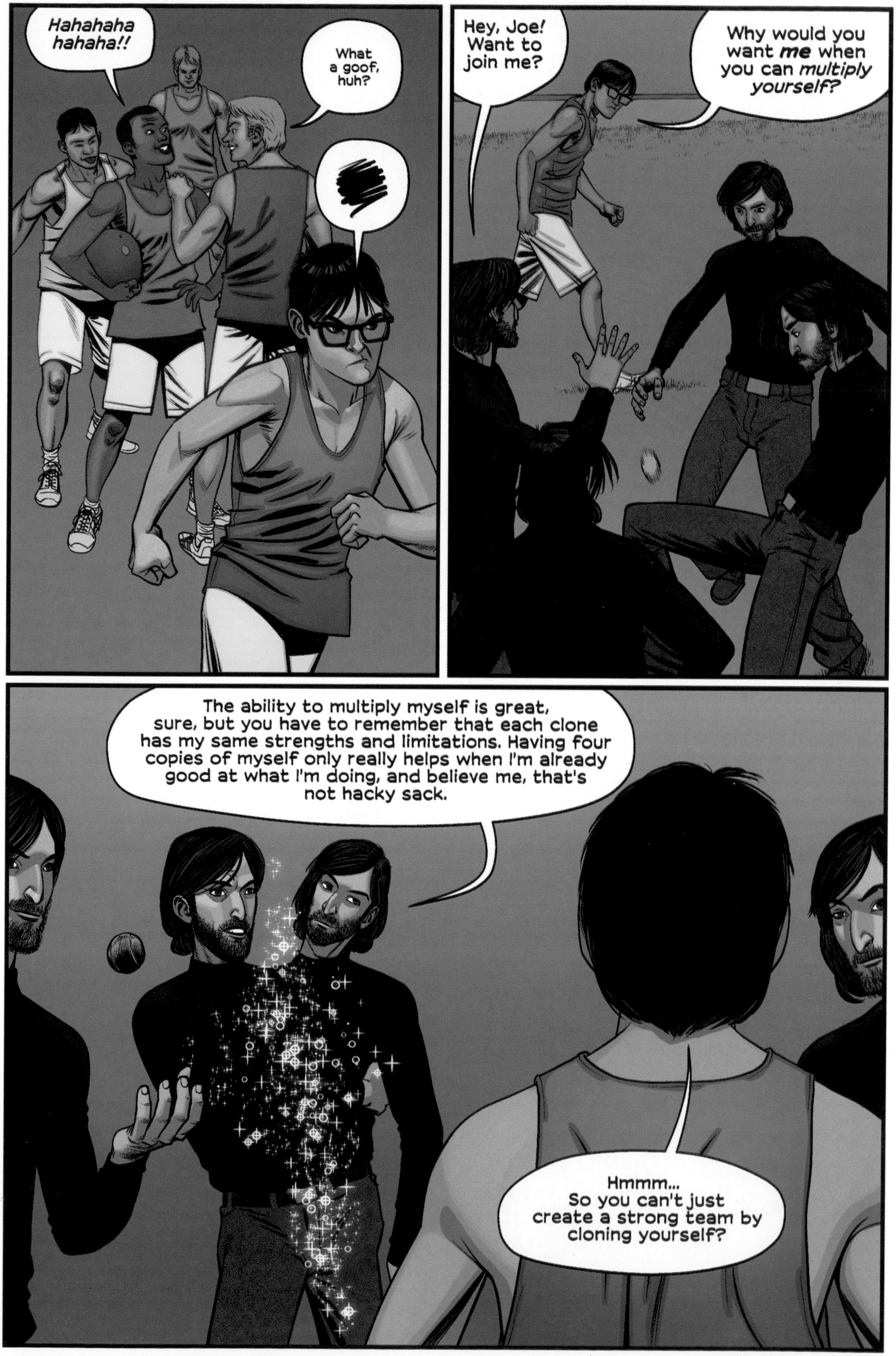
Hahahaha hahaha!!
What a goof, huh?
Hey, Joe! Want to join me?
Why would you want **me** when you can *multiply yourself?*
The ability to multiply myself is great, sure, but you have to remember that each clone has my same strengths and limitations. Having four copies of myself only really helps when I'm already good at what I'm doing, and believe me, that's not hacky sack.
Hmmm... So you can't just create a strong team by cloning yourself?

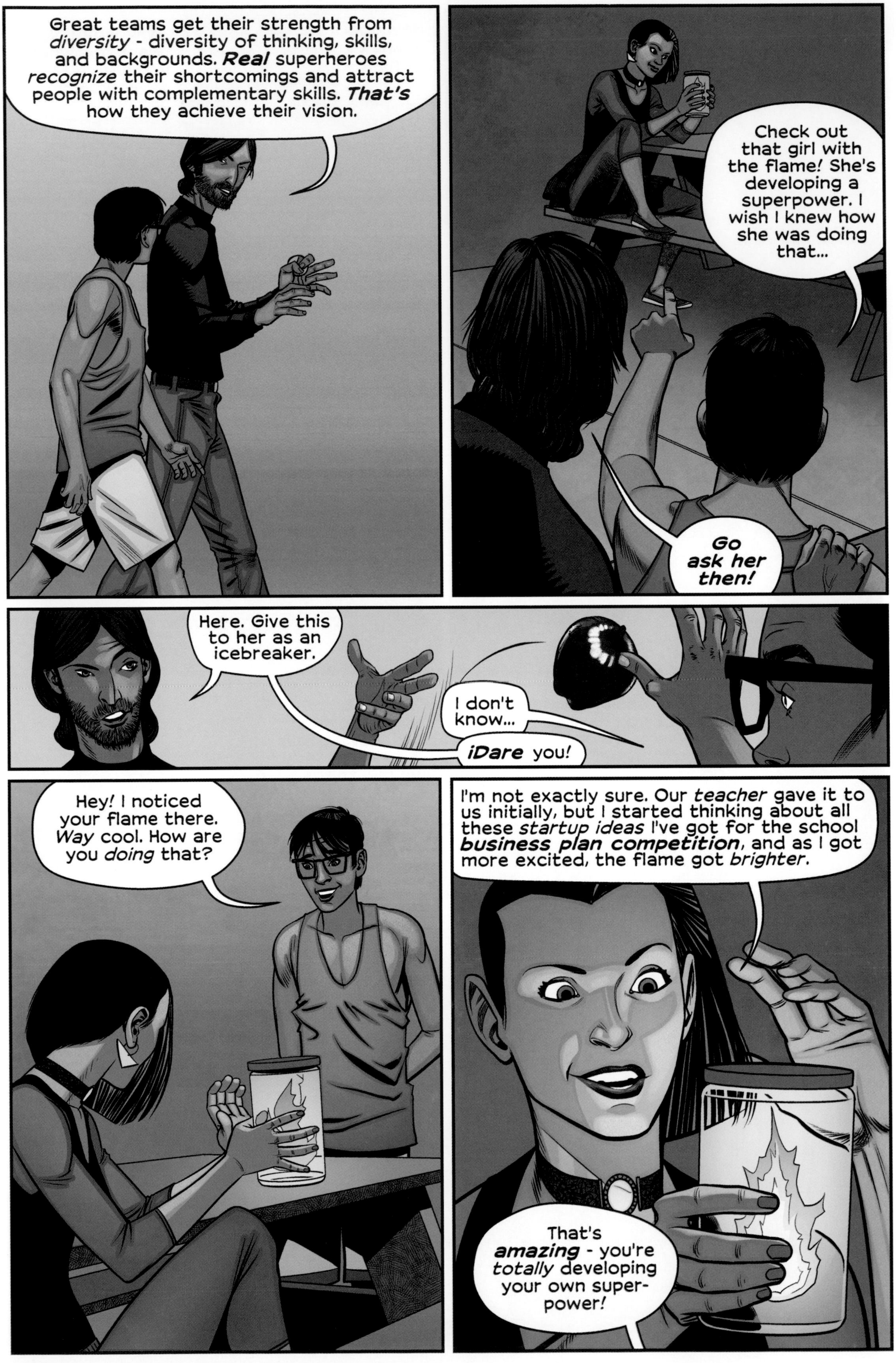
Great teams get their strength from *diversity* - diversity of thinking, skills, and backgrounds. ***Real*** superheroes *recognize* their shortcomings and attract people with complementary skills. ***That's*** how they achieve their vision.
Check out that girl with the flame! She's developing a superpower. I wish I knew how she was doing that...
Go ask her then!
Here. Give this to her as an icebreaker.
I don't know...
iDare you!
Hey! I noticed your flame there. *Way* cool. How are you *doing* that?
I'm not exactly sure. Our *teacher* gave it to us initially, but I started thinking about all these *startup ideas* I've got for the school ***business plan competition***, and as I got more excited, the flame got *brighter*.
That's ***amazing*** - you're *totally* developing your own super-power!

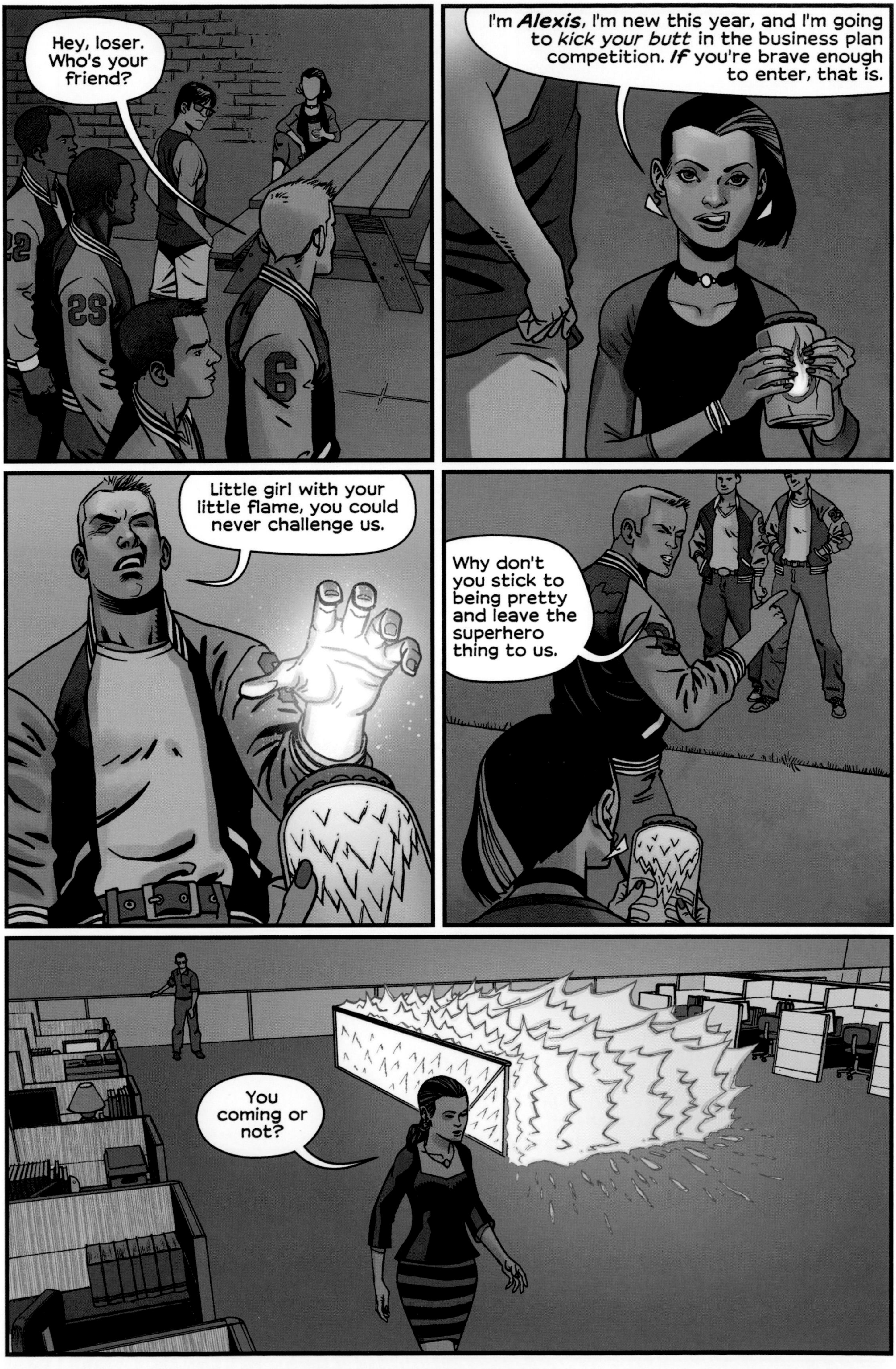
Hey, loser. Who's your friend?
I'm *Alexis*, I'm new this year, and I'm going to *kick your butt* in the business plan competition. *If* you're brave enough to enter, that is.
Little girl with your little flame, you could never challenge us.
Why don't you stick to being pretty and leave the superhero thing to us.
You coming or not?

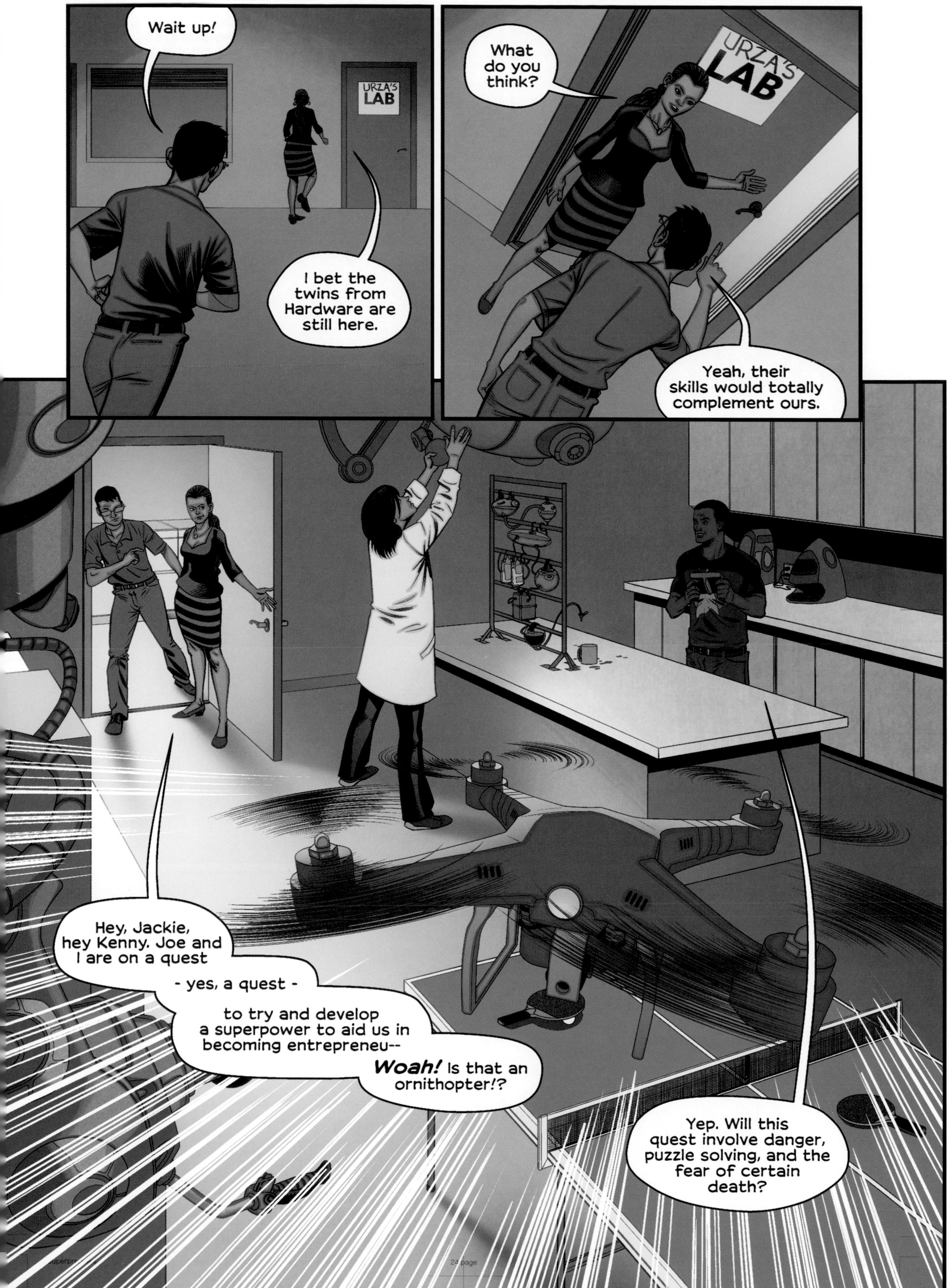
Wait up!
URZA'S LAB
I bet the twins from Hardware are still here.
URZA'S LAB
What do you think?
Yeah, their skills would totally complement ours.
Hey, Jackie, hey Kenny. Joe and I are on a quest
- yes, a quest -
to try and develop a superpower to aid us in becoming entrepreneu--
Woah! Is that an ornithopter!?
Yep. Will this quest involve danger, puzzle solving, and the fear of certain death?

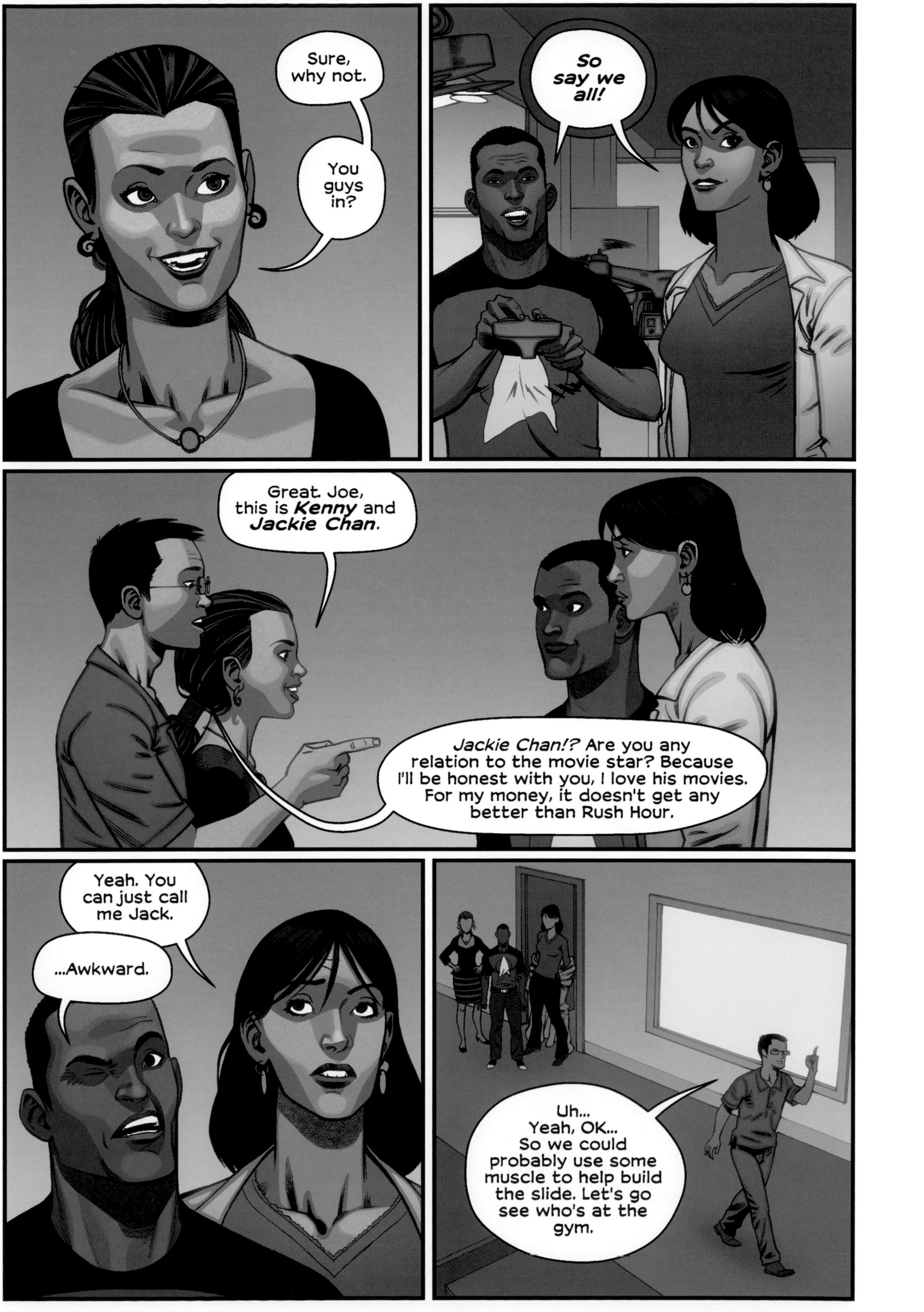
Sure, why not.
You guys in?
So say we all!
Great. Joe, this is ***Kenny*** and ***Jackie Chan***.
Jackie Chan!? Are you any relation to the movie star? Because I'll be honest with you, I love his movies. For my money, it doesn't get any better than Rush Hour.
Yeah. You can just call me Jack.
...Awkward.
Uh... Yeah, OK... So we could probably use some muscle to help build the slide. Let's go see who's at the gym.

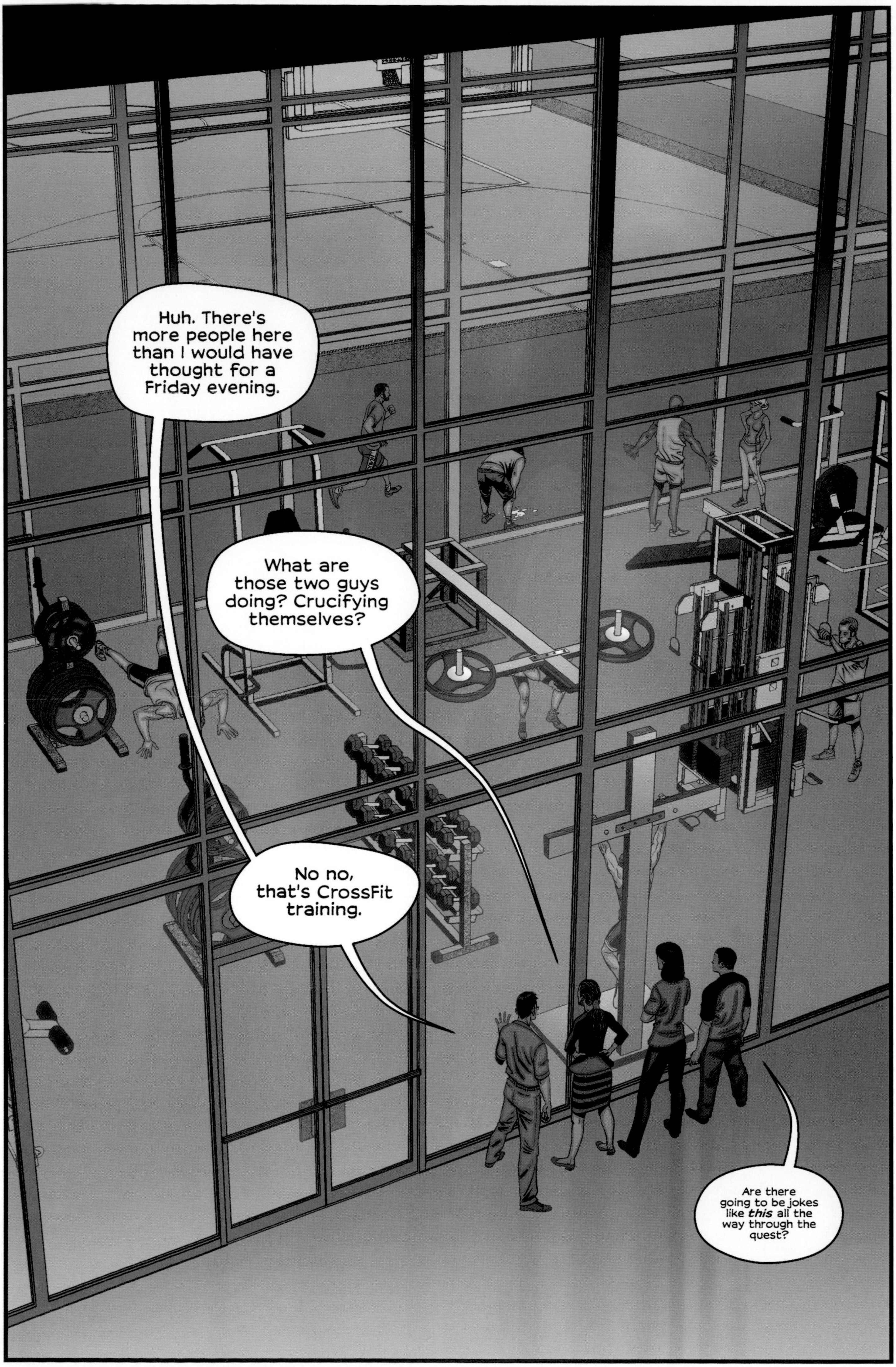
Huh. There's more people here than I would have thought for a Friday evening.
What are those two guys doing? Crucifying themselves?
No no, that's CrossFit training.
Are there going to be jokes like *this* all the way through the quest?

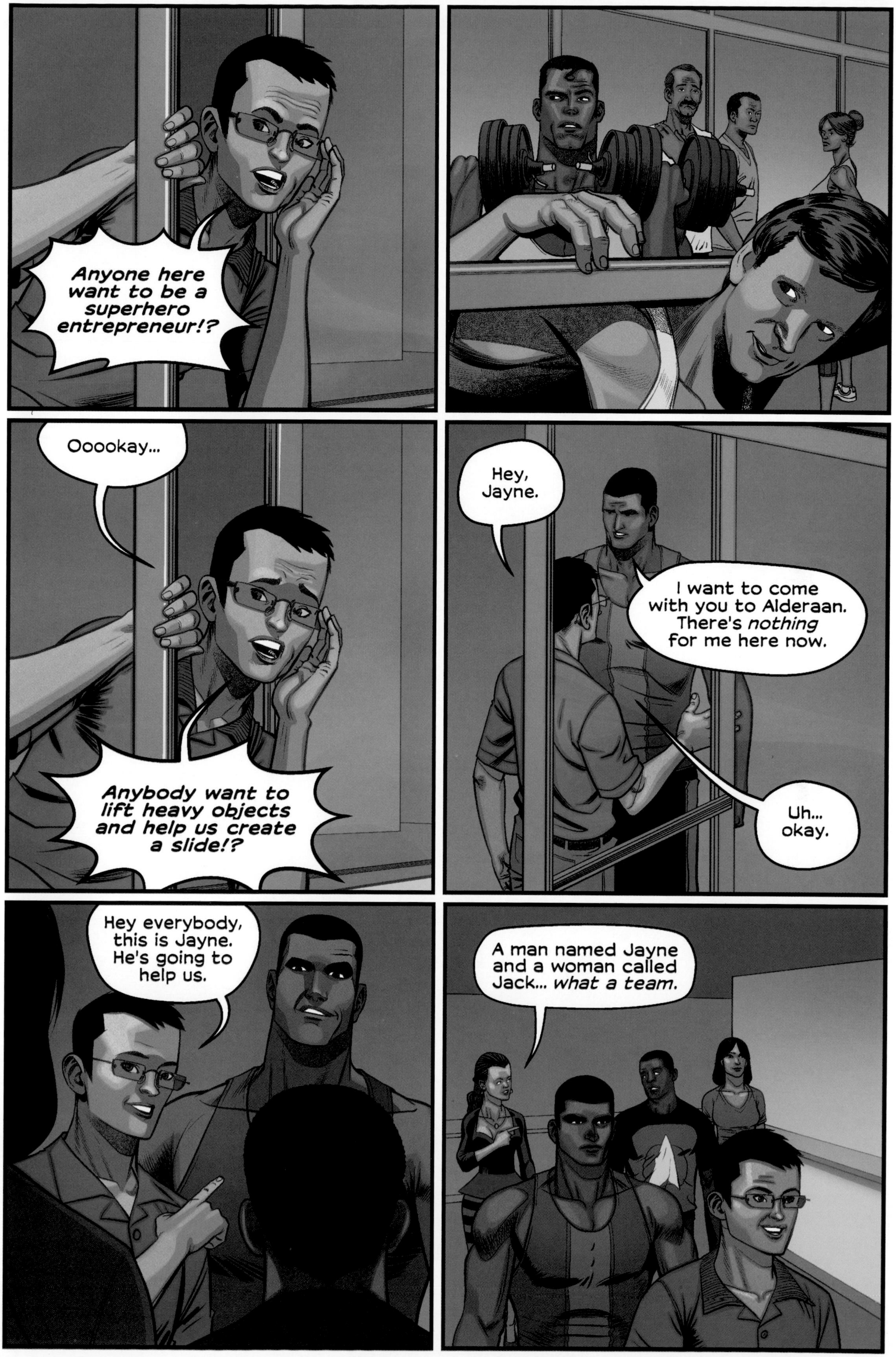
Anyone here want to be a superhero entrepreneur!?
Ooookay...
Anybody want to lift heavy objects and help us create a slide!?
Hey, Jayne.
I want to come with you to Alderaan. There's *nothing* for me here now.
Uh... okay.
Hey everybody, this is Jayne. He's going to help us.
A man named Jayne and a woman called Jack... *what a team.*

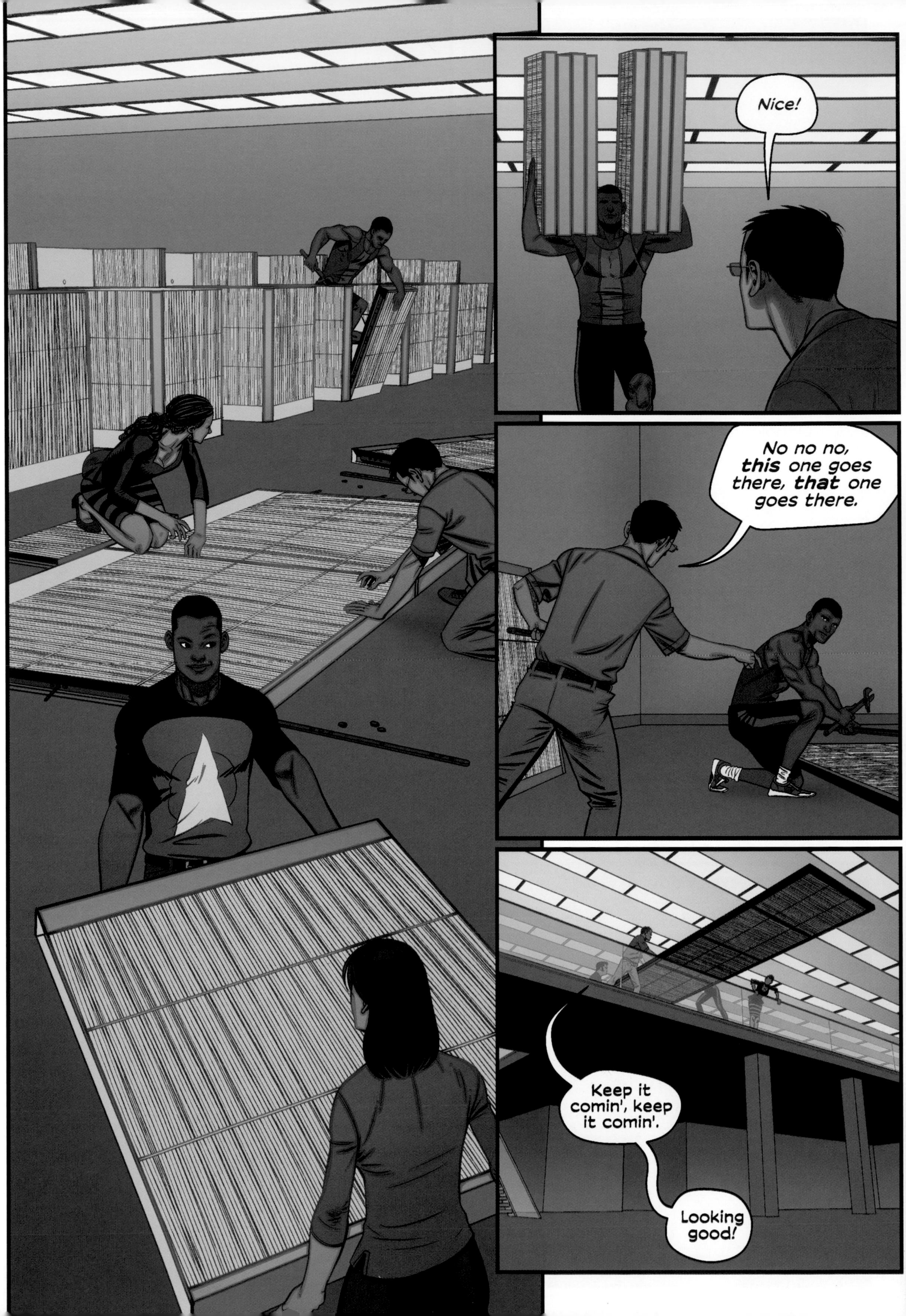

Nice!
No no no, **this** one goes there, **that** one goes there.
Keep it comin', keep it comin'.
Looking good!

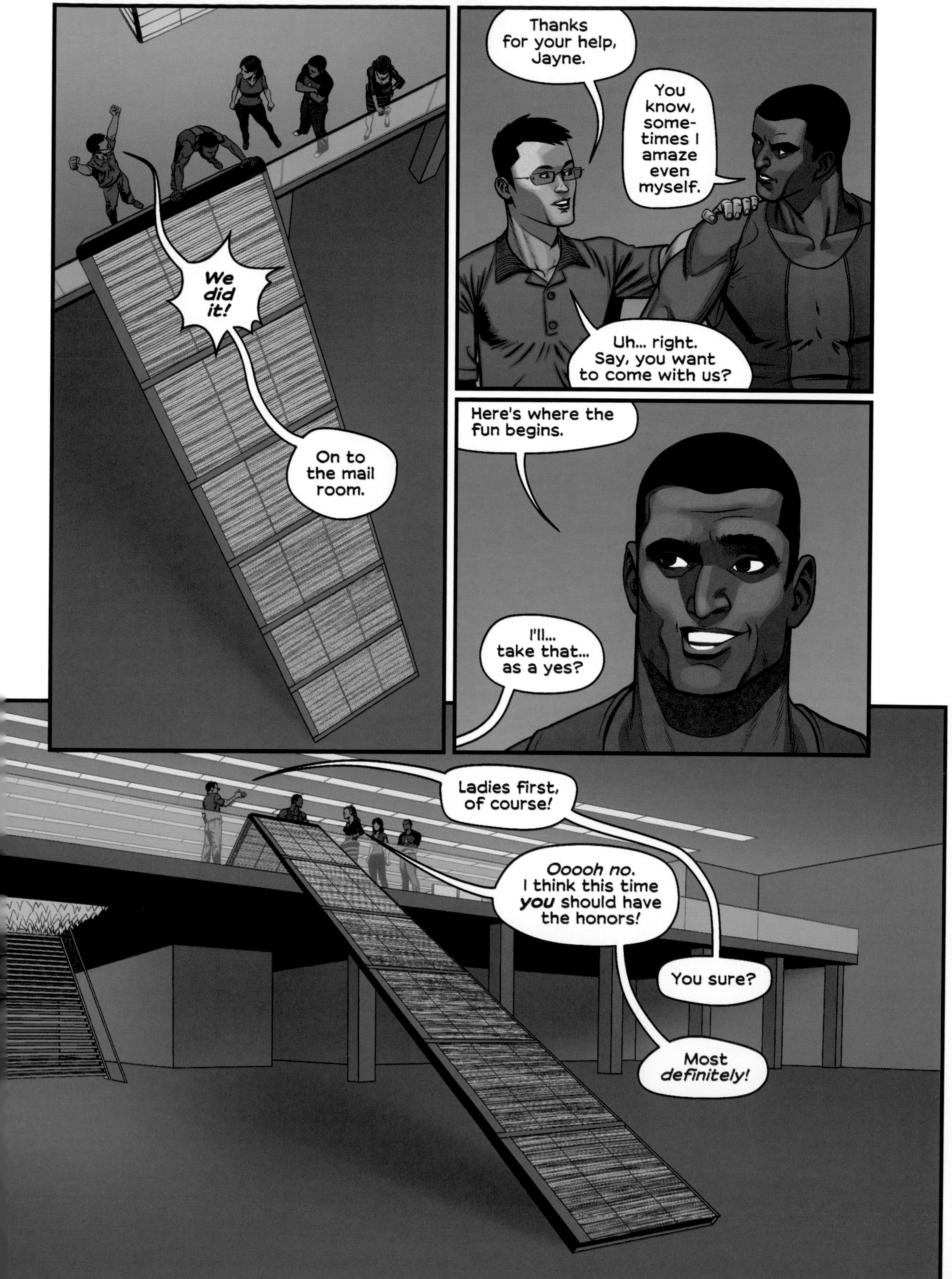
We did it!
On to the mail room.
Thanks for your help, Jayne.
You know, some-times I amaze even myself.
Uh... right. Say, you want to come with us?
Here's where the fun begins.
I'll... take that... as a yes?
Ladies first, of course!
Ooooh no. I think this time ***you*** should have the honors!
You sure?
Most *definitely!*

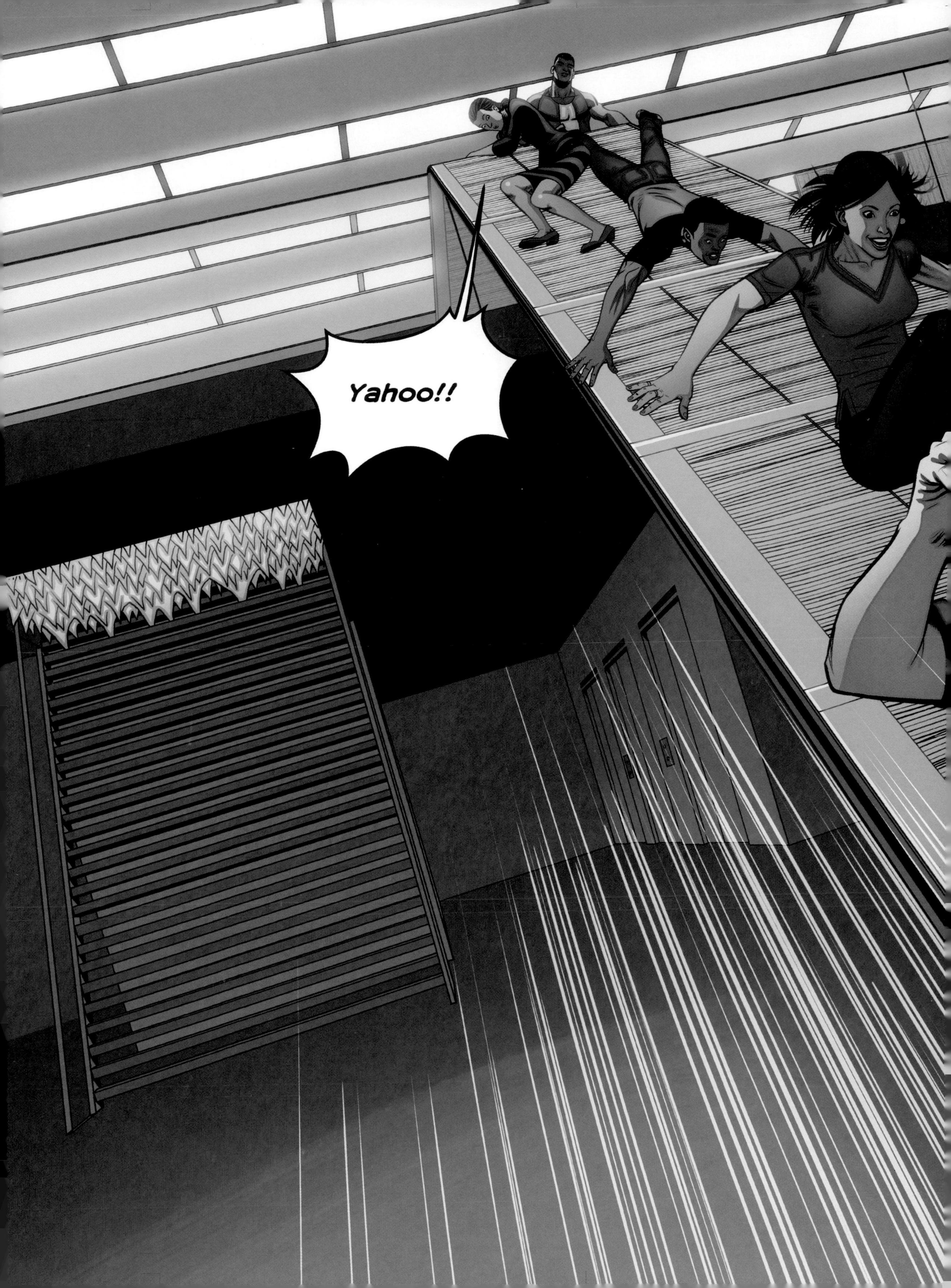
Yahoo!!

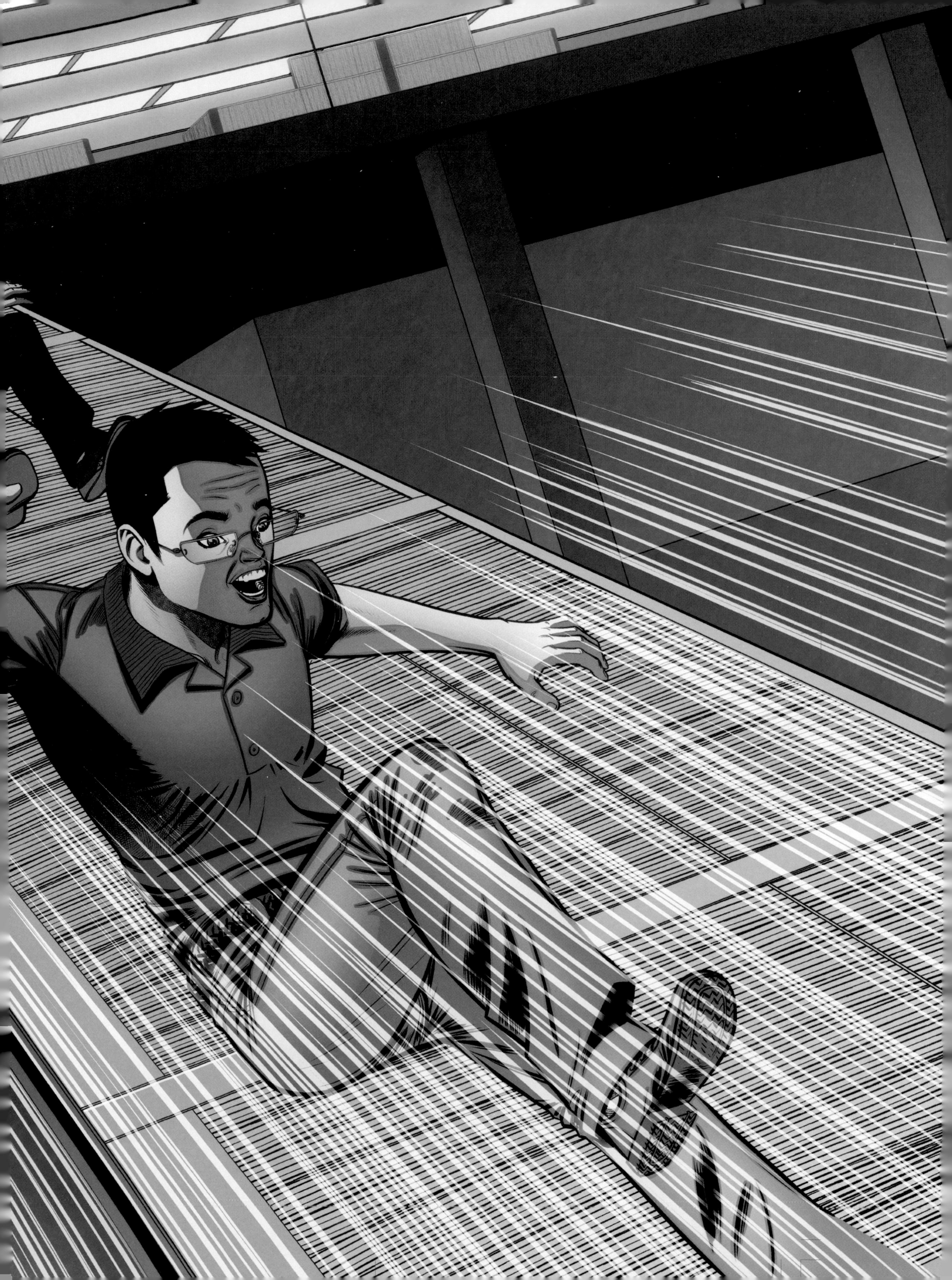

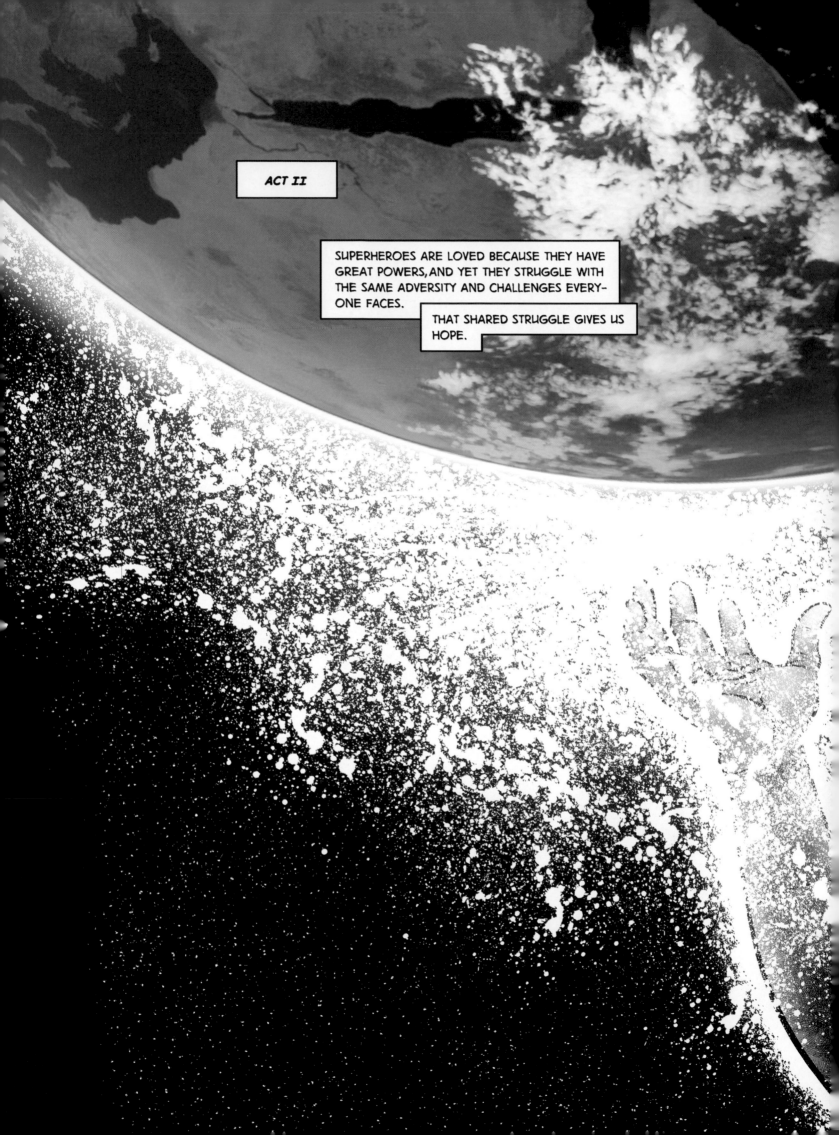

ACT II

SUPERHEROES ARE LOVED BECAUSE THEY HAVE GREAT POWERS, AND YET THEY STRUGGLE WITH THE SAME ADVERSITY AND CHALLENGES EVERYONE FACES.

THAT SHARED STRUGGLE GIVES US HOPE.

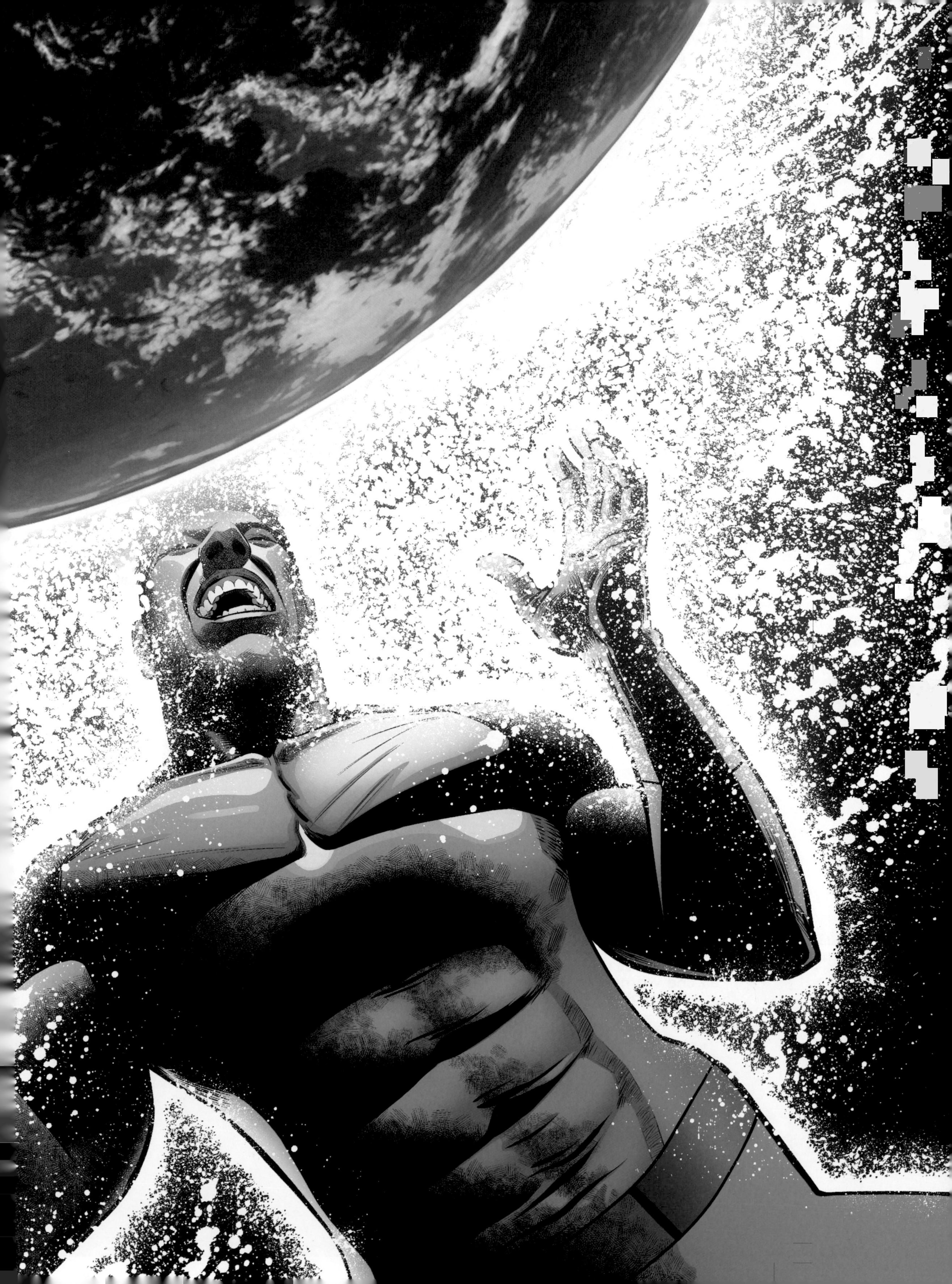

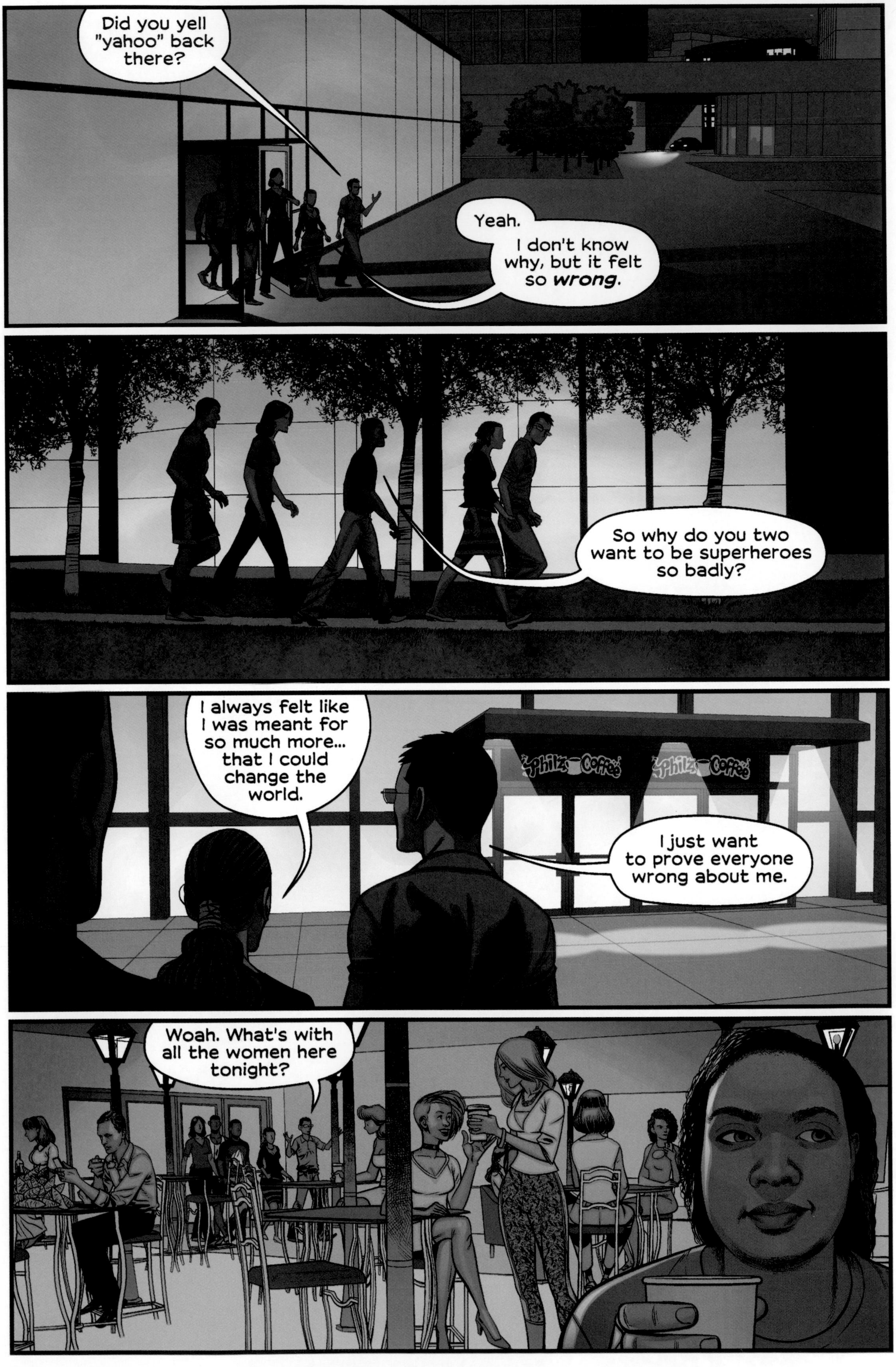
Did you yell "yahoo" back there?
Yeah.
I don't know why, but it felt so *wrong*.
So why do you two want to be superheroes so badly?
I always felt like I was meant for so much more... that I could change the world.
Philz Coffee
Philz Coffee
I just want to prove everyone wrong about me.
Woah. What's with all the women here tonight?

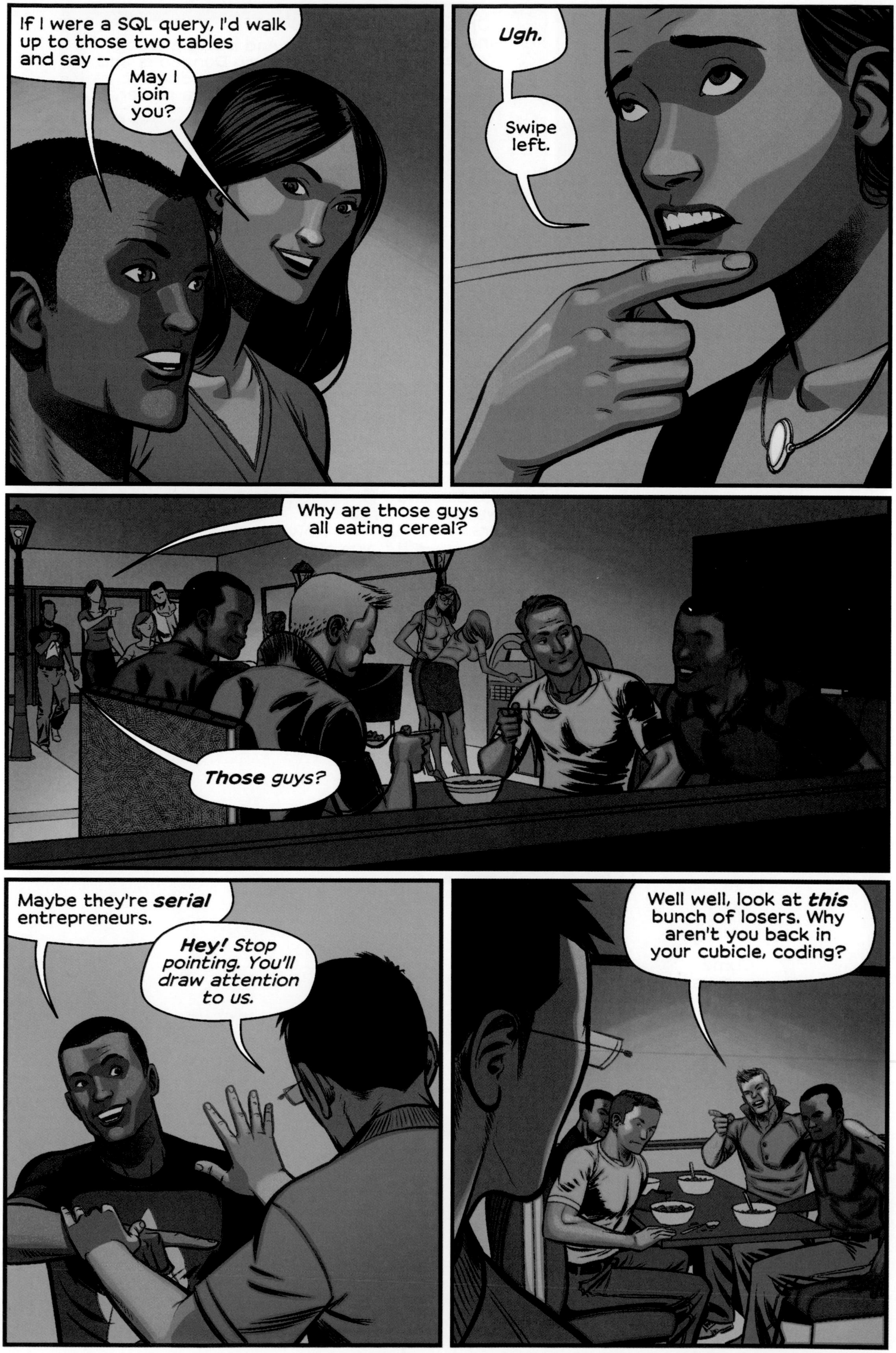
If I were a SQL query, I'd walk up to those two tables and say --
May I join you?
Ugh.
Swipe left.
Why are those guys all eating cereal?
Those guys?
Maybe they're *serial* entrepreneurs.
Hey! Stop pointing. You'll draw attention to us.
Well well, look at *this* bunch of losers. Why aren't you back in your cubicle, coding?

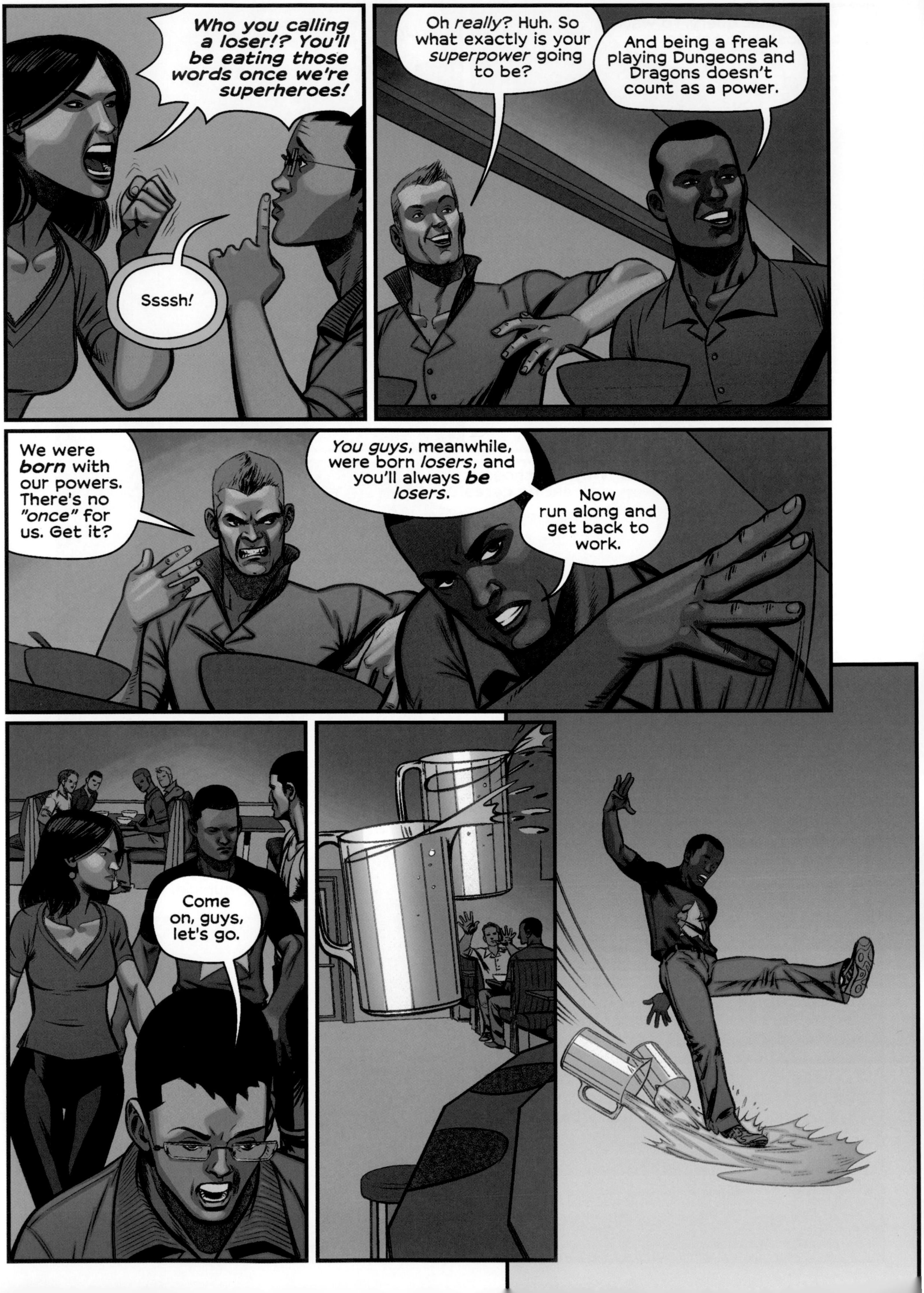
Who you calling a loser!? You'll be eating those words once we're superheroes!
Ssssh!
Oh really? Huh. So what exactly is your superpower going to be?
And being a freak playing Dungeons and Dragons doesn't count as a power.
We were born with our powers. There's no "once" for us. Get it?
You guys, meanwhile, were born losers, and you'll always be losers.
Now run along and get back to work.
Come on, guys, let's go.

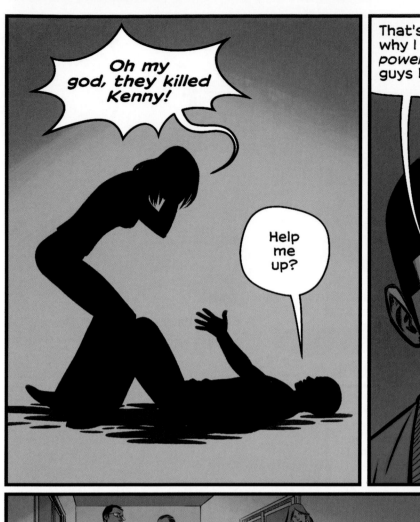

Oh my god, they killed Kenny!

Help me up?

That's *exactly* why I want *super powers*, to stop guys like *that*.

But what makes you think you wouldn't become a villain, like them?

You really think I could become evil?

Well, not generally, but how can anyone really know?

What's all this?

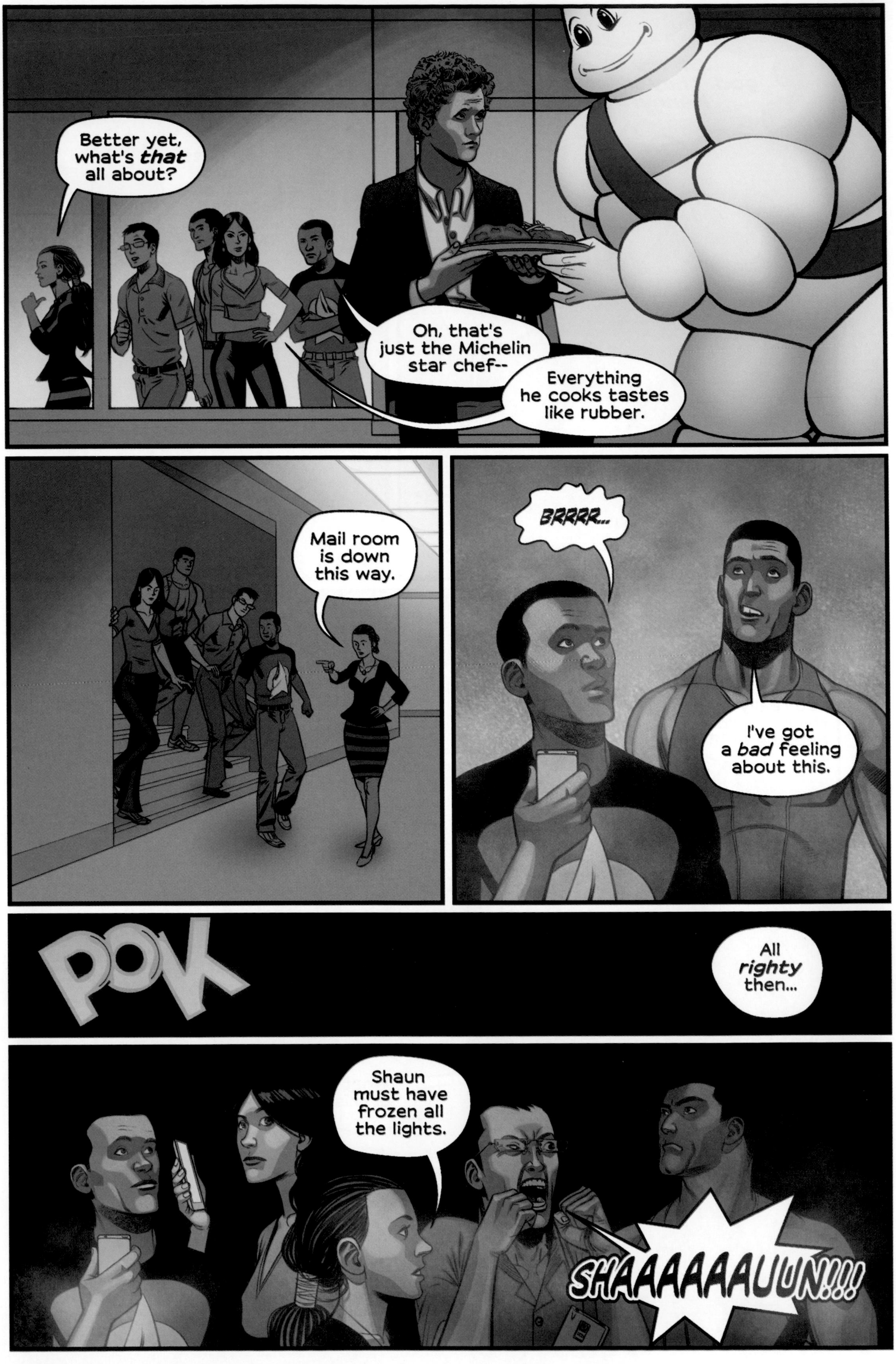
Better yet, what's *that* all about?
Oh, that's just the Michelin star chef--
Everything he cooks tastes like rubber.
Mail room is down this way.
BRRRR...
I've got a *bad* feeling about this.
POK
All *righty* then...
Shaun must have frozen all the lights.
SHAAAAAAUUN!!!

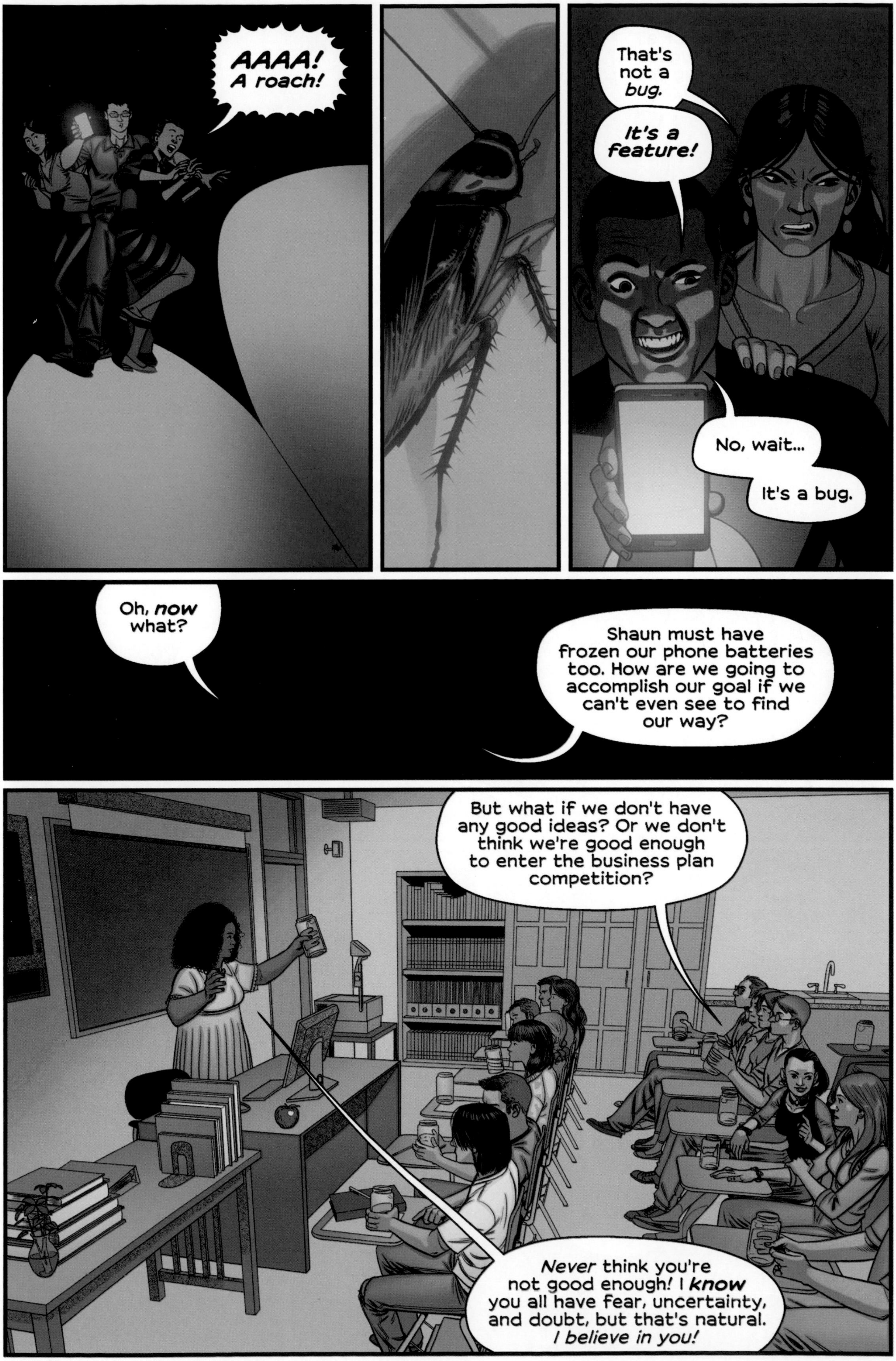
AAAA! A roach!
That's not a bug.
It's a feature!
No, wait...
It's a bug.
Oh, now what?
Shaun must have frozen our phone batteries too. How are we going to accomplish our goal if we can't even see to find our way?
But what if we don't have any good ideas? Or we don't think we're good enough to enter the business plan competition?
Never think you're not good enough! I know you all have fear, uncertainty, and doubt, but that's natural. I believe in you!

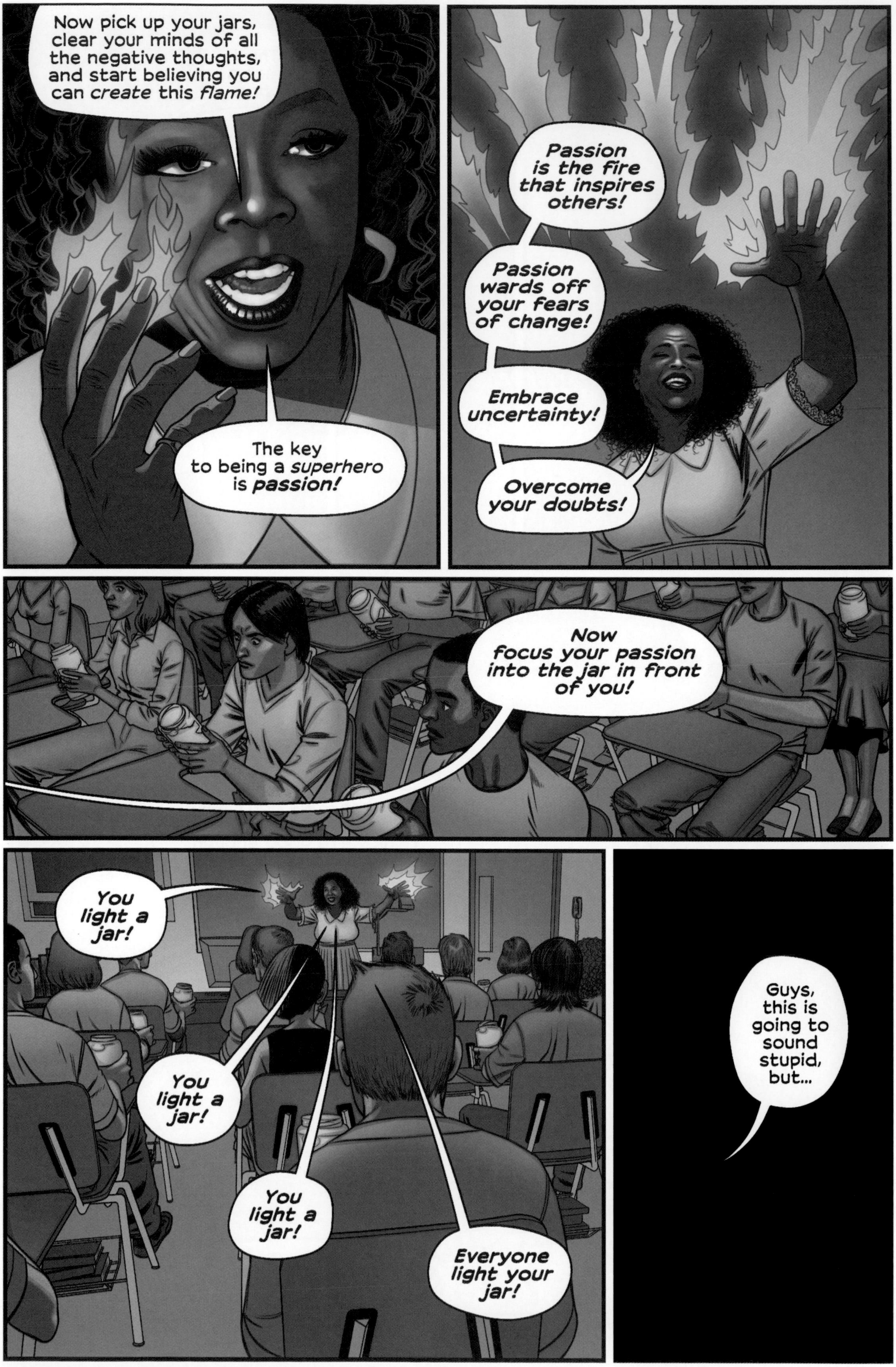
Now pick up your jars, clear your minds of all the negative thoughts, and start believing you can *create* this *flame!*
The key to being a *superhero* is ***passion!***
Passion is the fire that inspires others!
Passion wards off your fears of change!
Embrace uncertainty!
Overcome your doubts!
Now focus your passion into the jar in front of you!
You light a jar!
You light a jar!
You light a jar!
Everyone light your jar!
Guys, this is going to sound stupid, but...

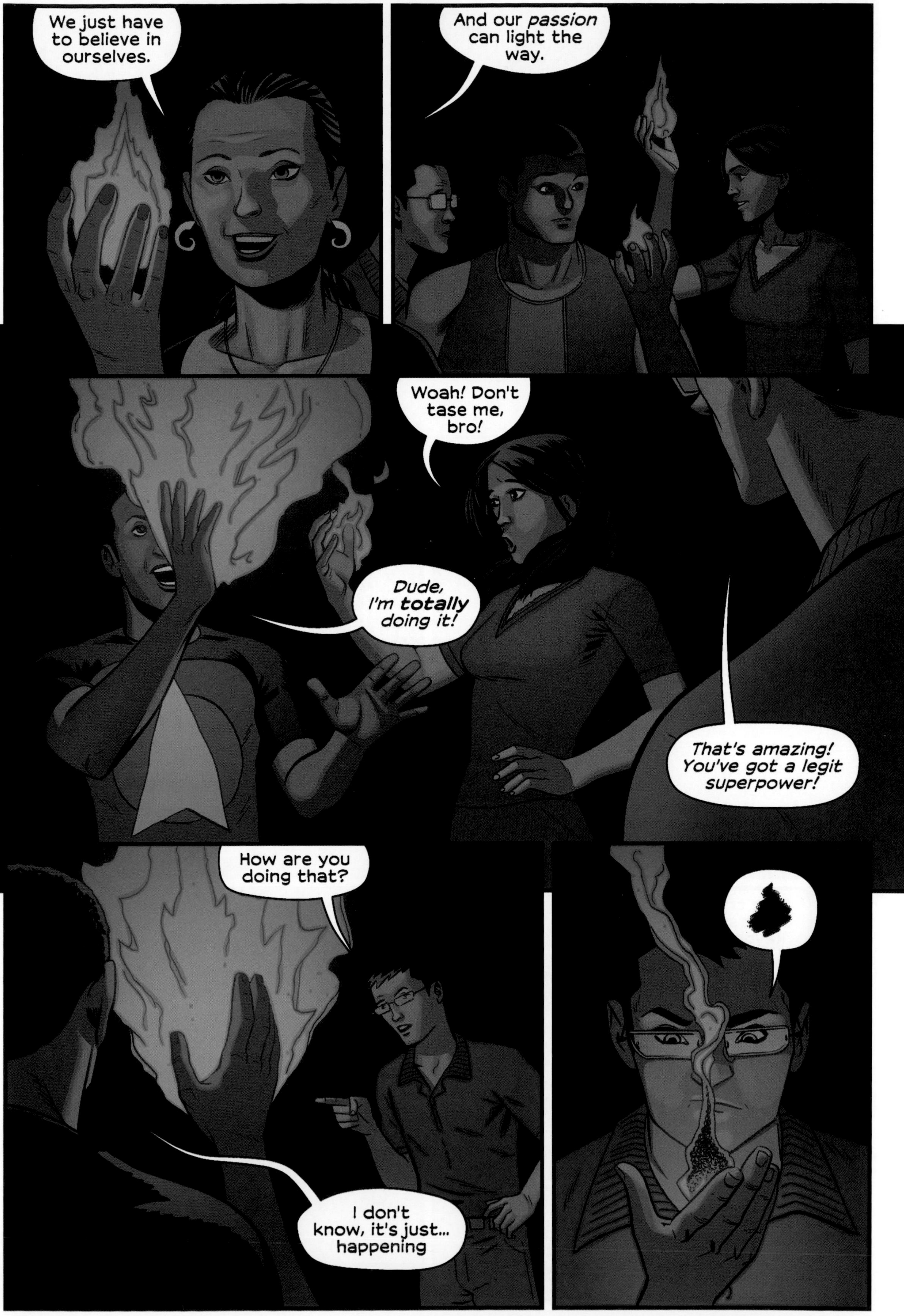
We just have to believe in ourselves.
And our *passion* can light the way.
Woah! Don't tase me, bro!
*Dude, I'm **totally** doing it!*
That's amazing! You've got a legit superpower!
How are you doing that?
I don't know, it's just... happening

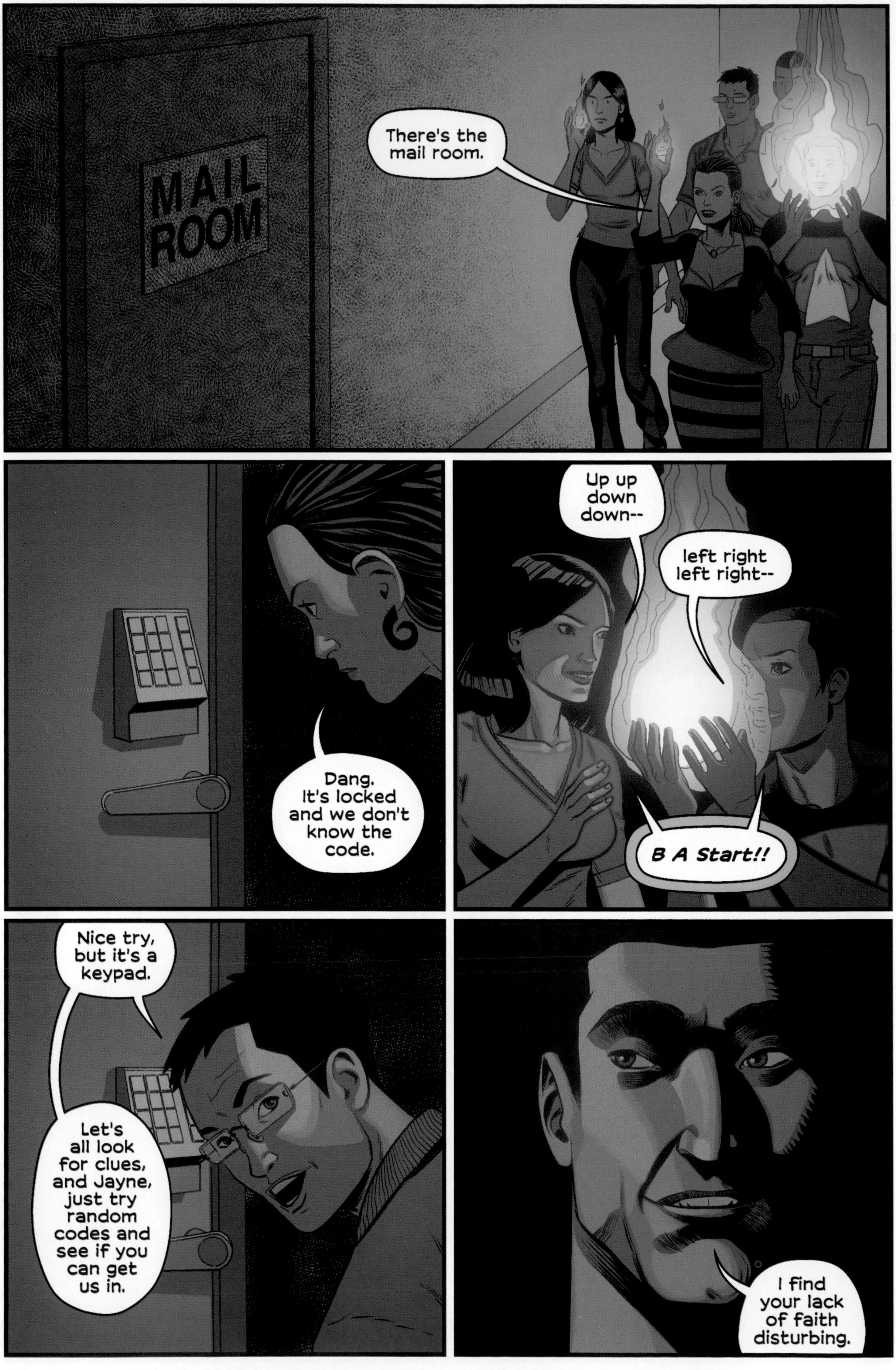
MAIL ROOM
There's the mail room.
Dang. It's locked and we don't know the code.
Up up down down--
left right left right--
B A Start!!
Nice try, but it's a keypad.
Let's all look for clues, and Jayne, just try random codes and see if you can get us in.
I find your lack of faith disturbing.

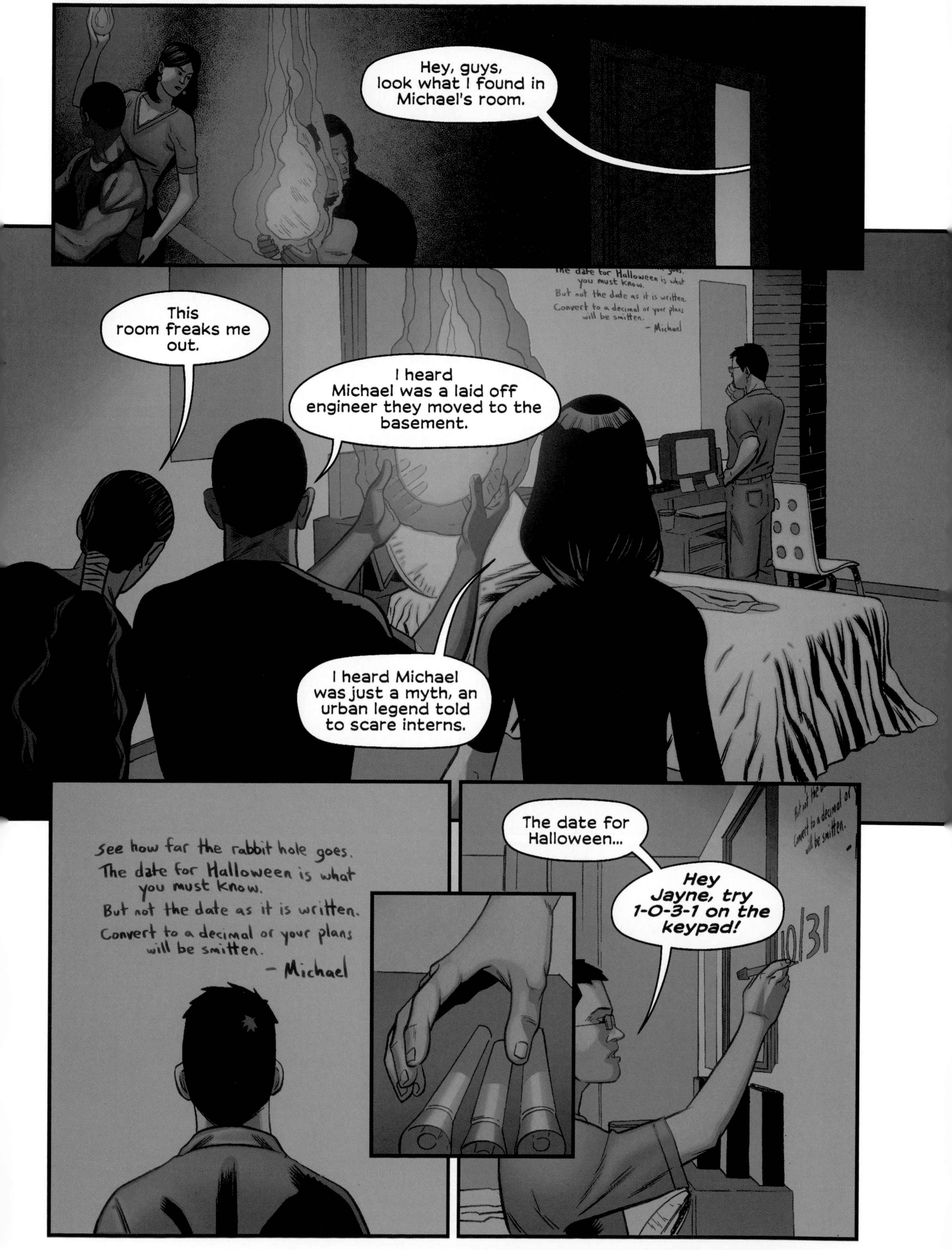

Hey, guys, look what I found in Michael's room.
The date for Halloween is what you must know. But not the date as it is written. Convert to a decimal or your plans will be smitten. – Michael
This room freaks me out.
I heard Michael was a laid off engineer they moved to the basement.
I heard Michael was just a myth, an urban legend told to scare interns.
See how far the rabbit hole goes. The date for Halloween is what you must know. But not the date as it is written. Convert to a decimal or your plans will be smitten. – Michael
The date for Halloween...
Hey Jayne, try 1-0-3-1 on the keypad!
10/31

...t hole goes.
...een is what

...t is written.
...or your plans

— Michael 10/31

Try not

...abbit hole goes
...loween is what
...low.
...as

...M...ael 10/31

Is that a "no"?

Do, or do not.

What!?

There is no try.

That's a "no"! Let's keep looking.

Boring conversation anyways...

There are 10 kinds of people in this world: Those who know binary code and those who do not.

What about this other message?

You don't think...

Totally!!

What?

"Oct 31" is the way Halloween is usually written.

And you can interpret that as "octal 31," which is 31 in base 8.

Oct 31

Octal 31

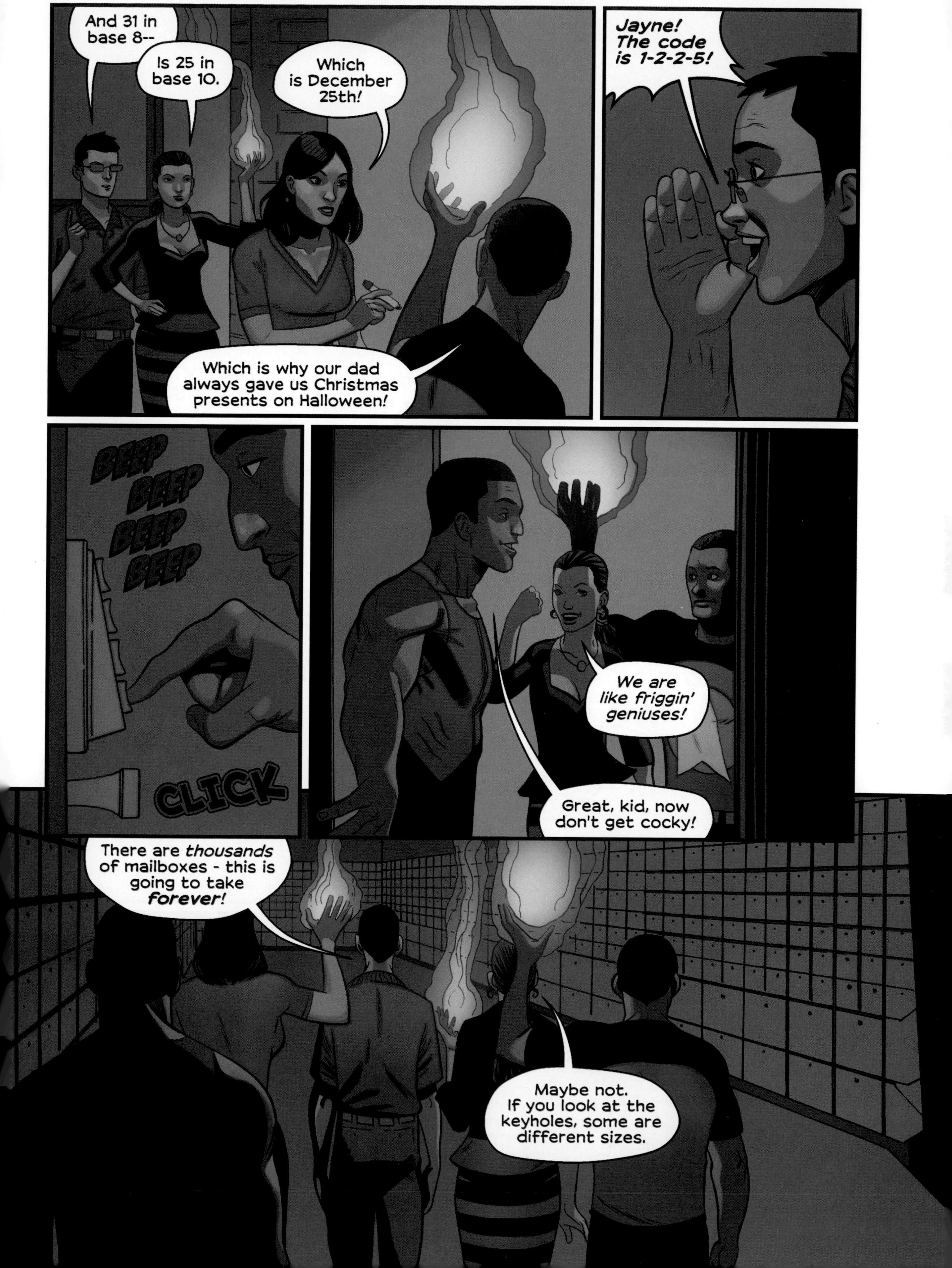
And 31 in base 8--
Is 25 in base 10.
Which is December 25th!
Which is why our dad always gave us Christmas presents on Halloween!
Jayne! The code is 1-2-2-5!
BEEP BEEP BEEP BEEP
CLICK
We are like friggin' geniuses!
Great, kid, now don't get cocky!
There are *thousands* of mailboxes - this is going to take ***forever***!
Maybe not. If you look at the keyholes, some are different sizes.

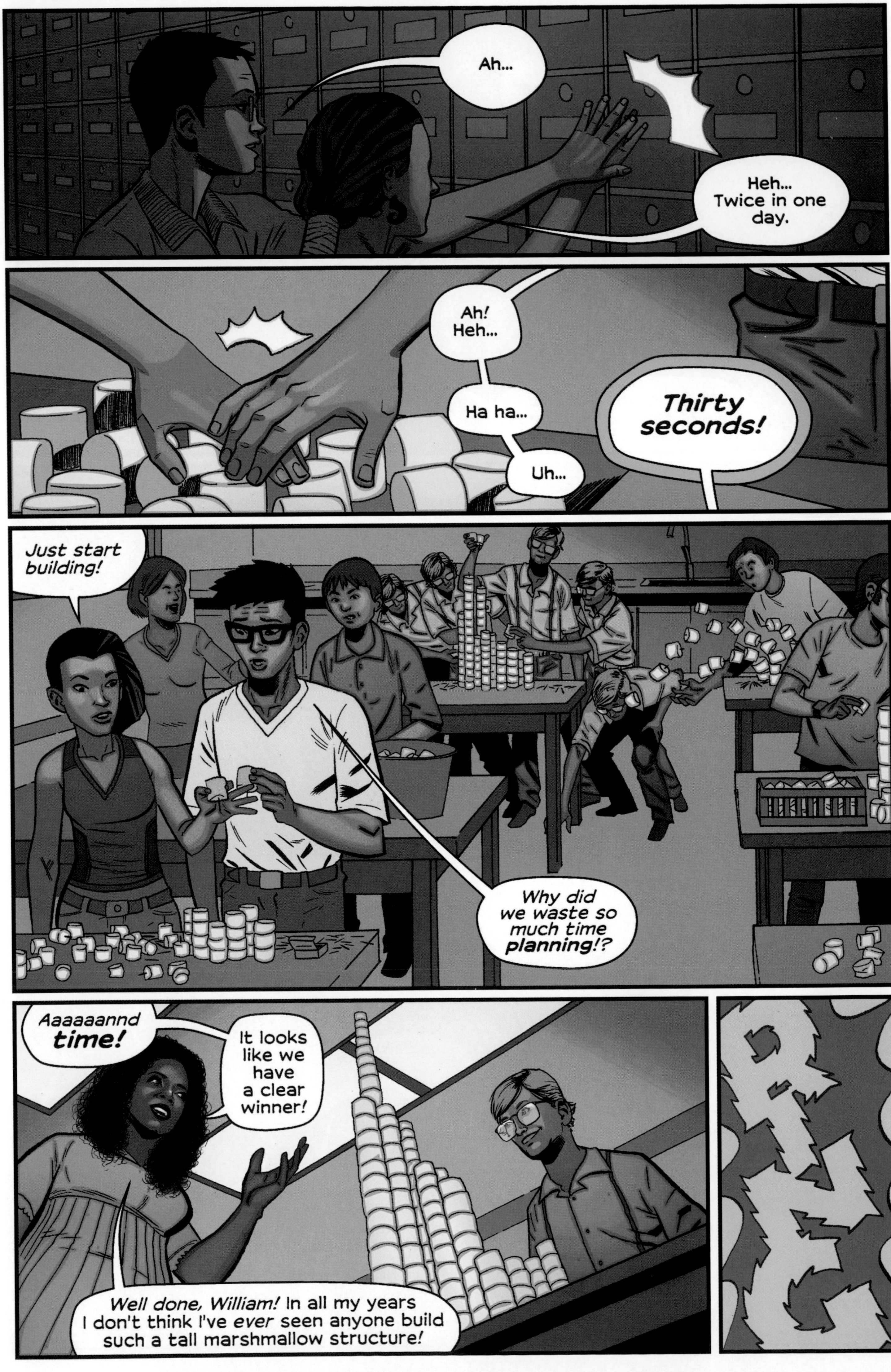
Ah...
Heh... Twice in one day.
Ah! Heh...
Ha ha...
Uh...
Thirty seconds!
Just start building!
Why did we waste so much time planning!?
Aaaaaannd time!
It looks like we have a clear winner!
Well done, William! In all my years I don't think I've ever seen anyone build such a tall marshmallow structure!

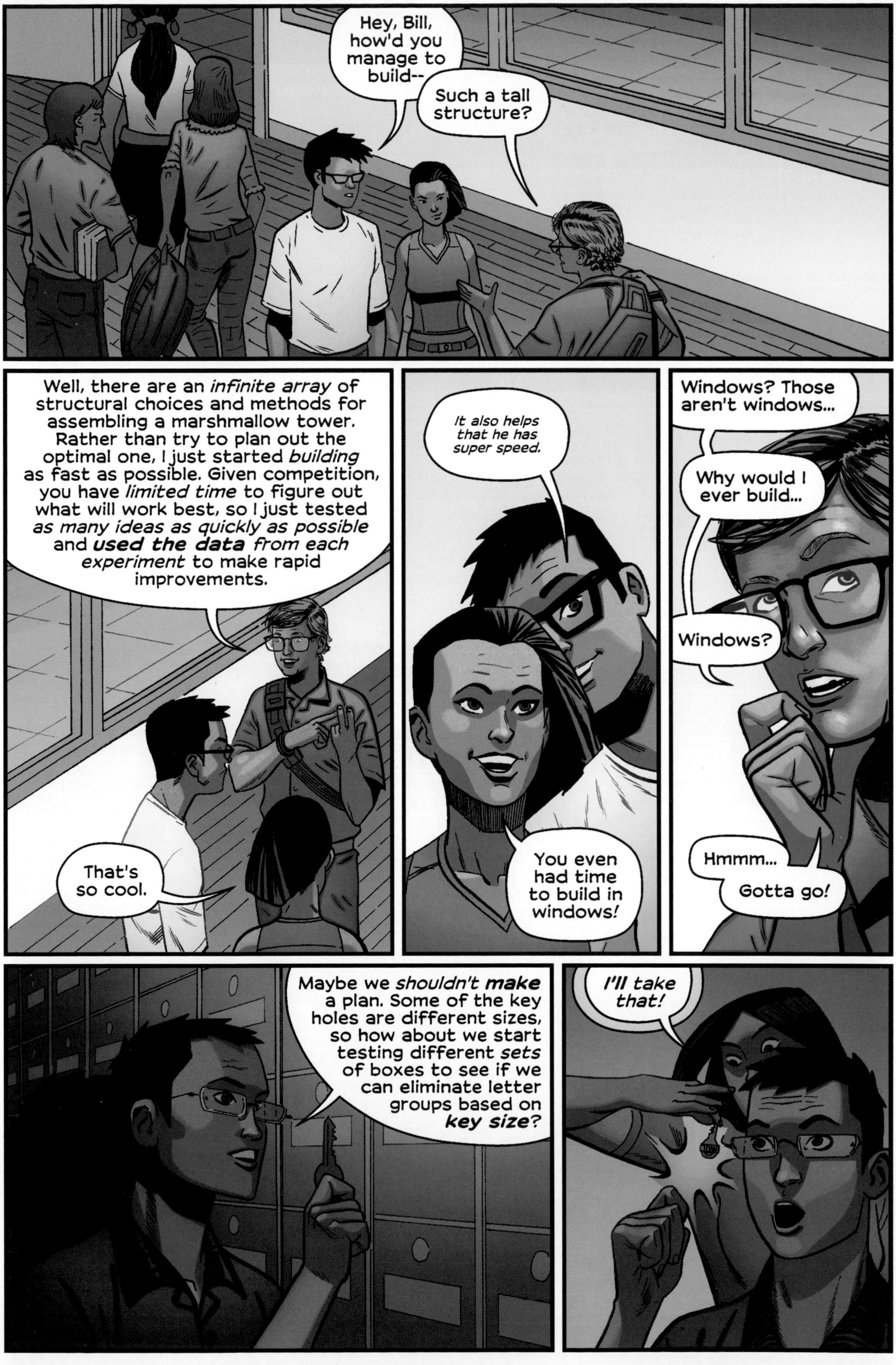
Hey, Bill, how'd you manage to build--
Such a tall structure?
Well, there are an *infinite array* of structural choices and methods for assembling a marshmallow tower. Rather than try to plan out the optimal one, I just started *building* as fast as possible. Given competition, you have *limited time* to figure out what will work best, so I just tested *as many ideas as quickly as possible* and ***used the data*** *from each experiment* to make rapid improvements.
That's so cool.
It also helps that he has super speed.
You even had time to build in windows*!*
Windows? Those aren't windows...
Why would I ever build...
Windows?
Hmmm...
Gotta go*!*
Maybe we *shouldn't* **make** a plan. Some of the key holes are different sizes, so how about we start testing different *sets* of boxes to see if we can eliminate letter groups based on ***key size***?
***I'll** take that!*

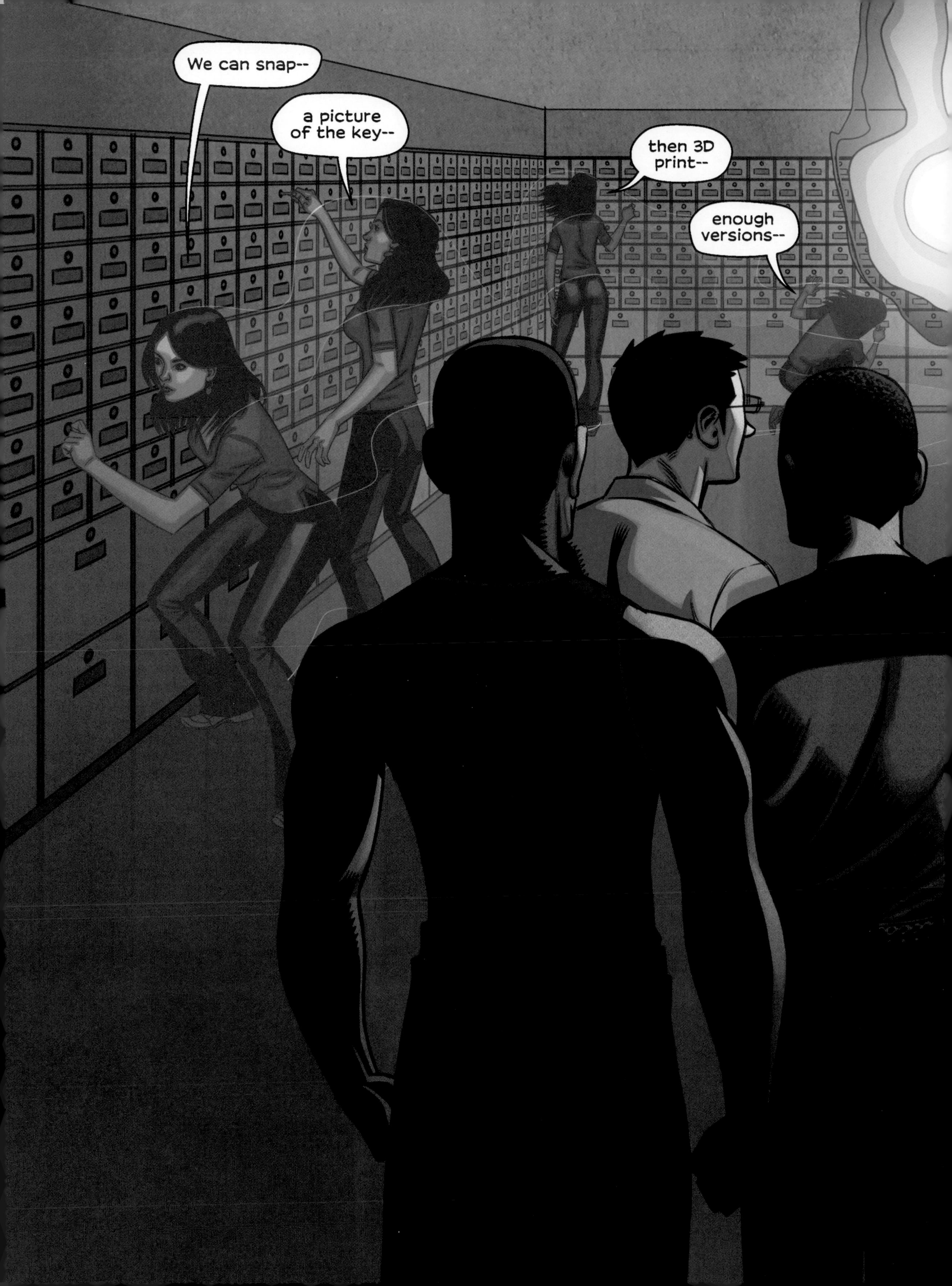
We can snap--
a picture of the key--
then 3D print--
enough versions--

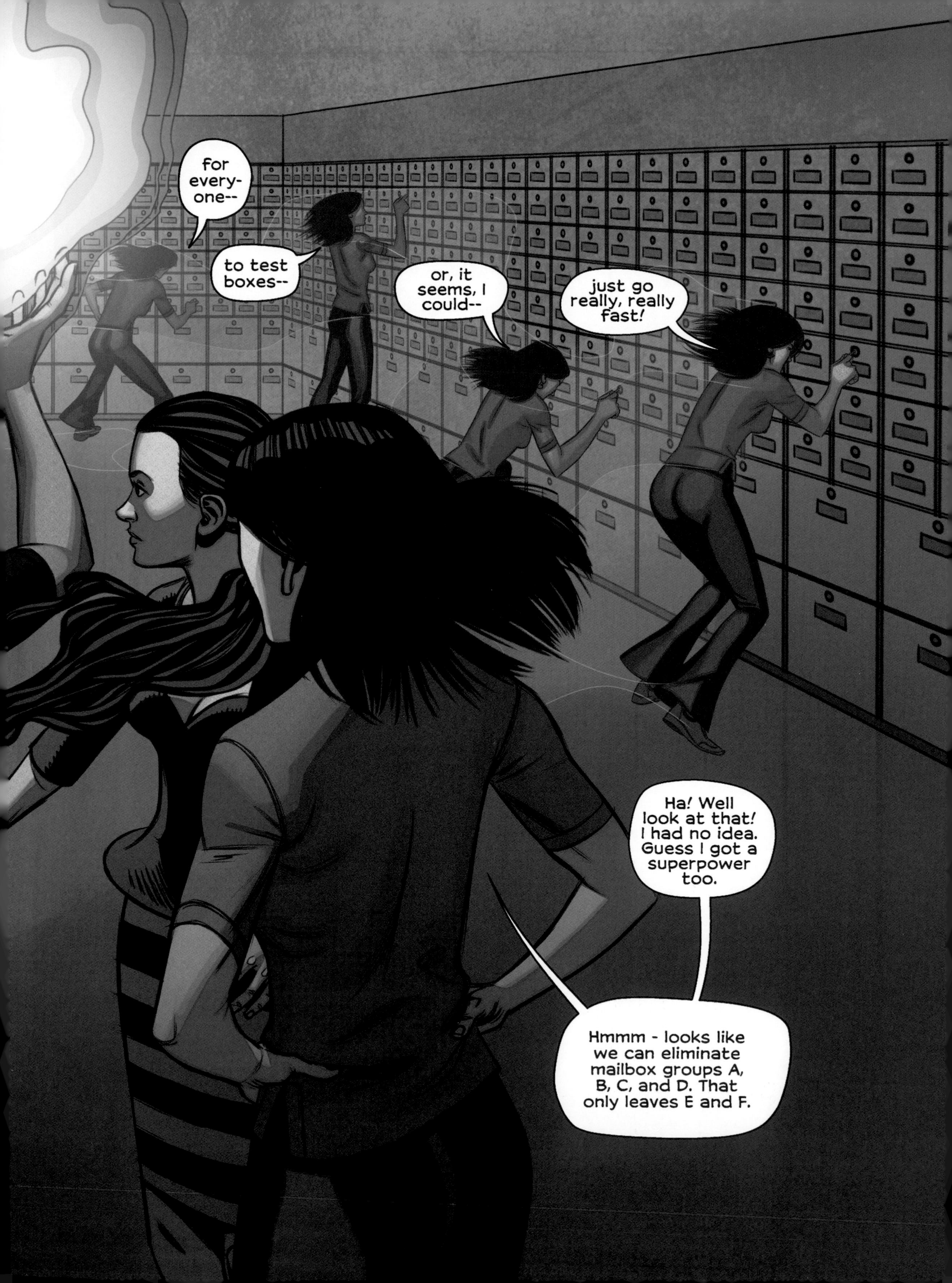
for every-one--
to test boxes--
or, it seems, I could--
just go really, really fast!
Ha! Well look at that! I had no idea. Guess I got a superpower too.
Hmmm - looks like we can eliminate mailbox groups A, B, C, and D. That only leaves E and F.

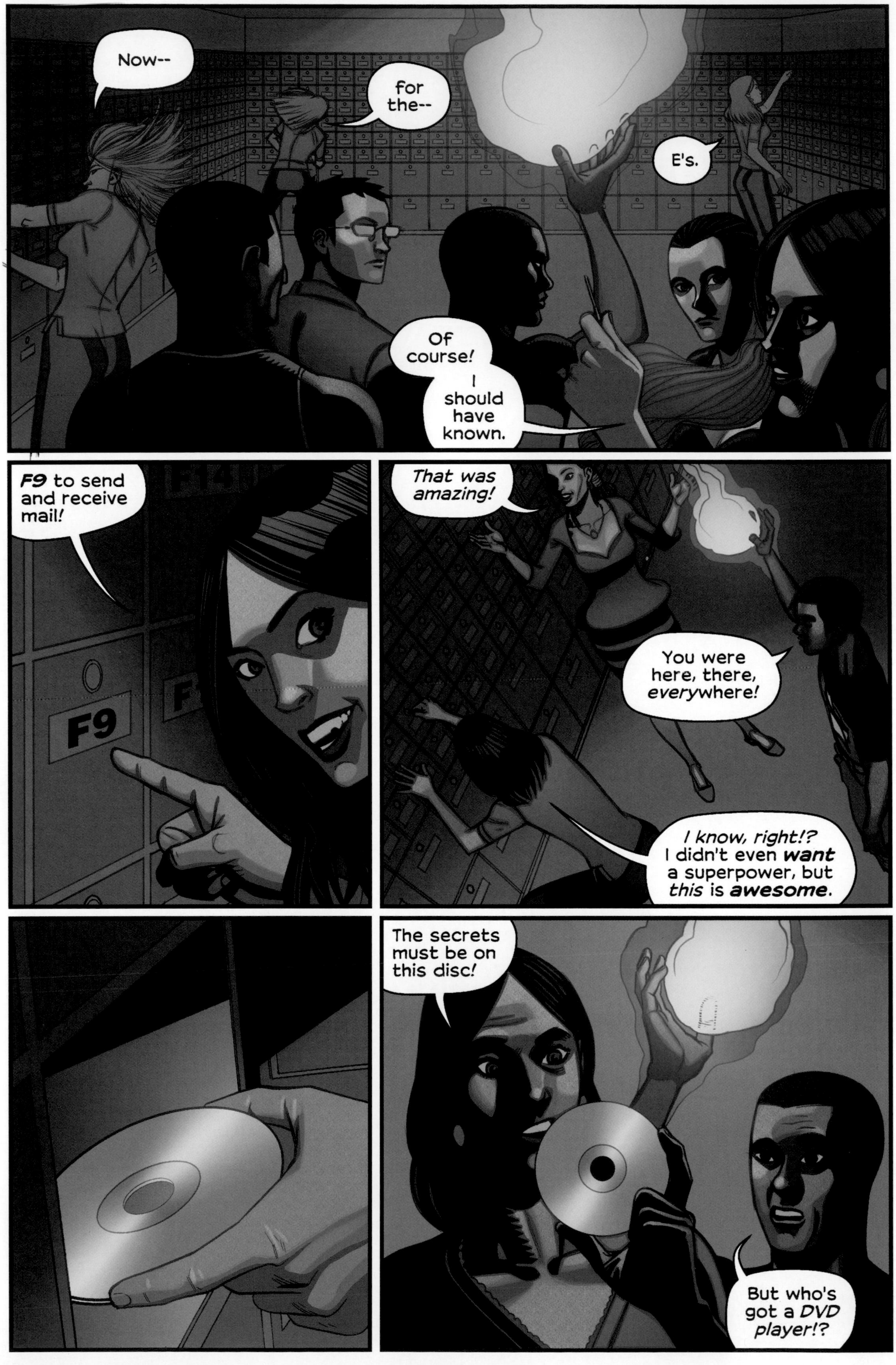
Now--
for the--
E's.
Of course!
I should have known.
F9 to send and receive mail!
F9
That was amazing!
You were here, there, everywhere!
I know, right!? I didn't even want a superpower, but this is awesome.
The secrets must be on this disc!
But who's got a DVD player!?

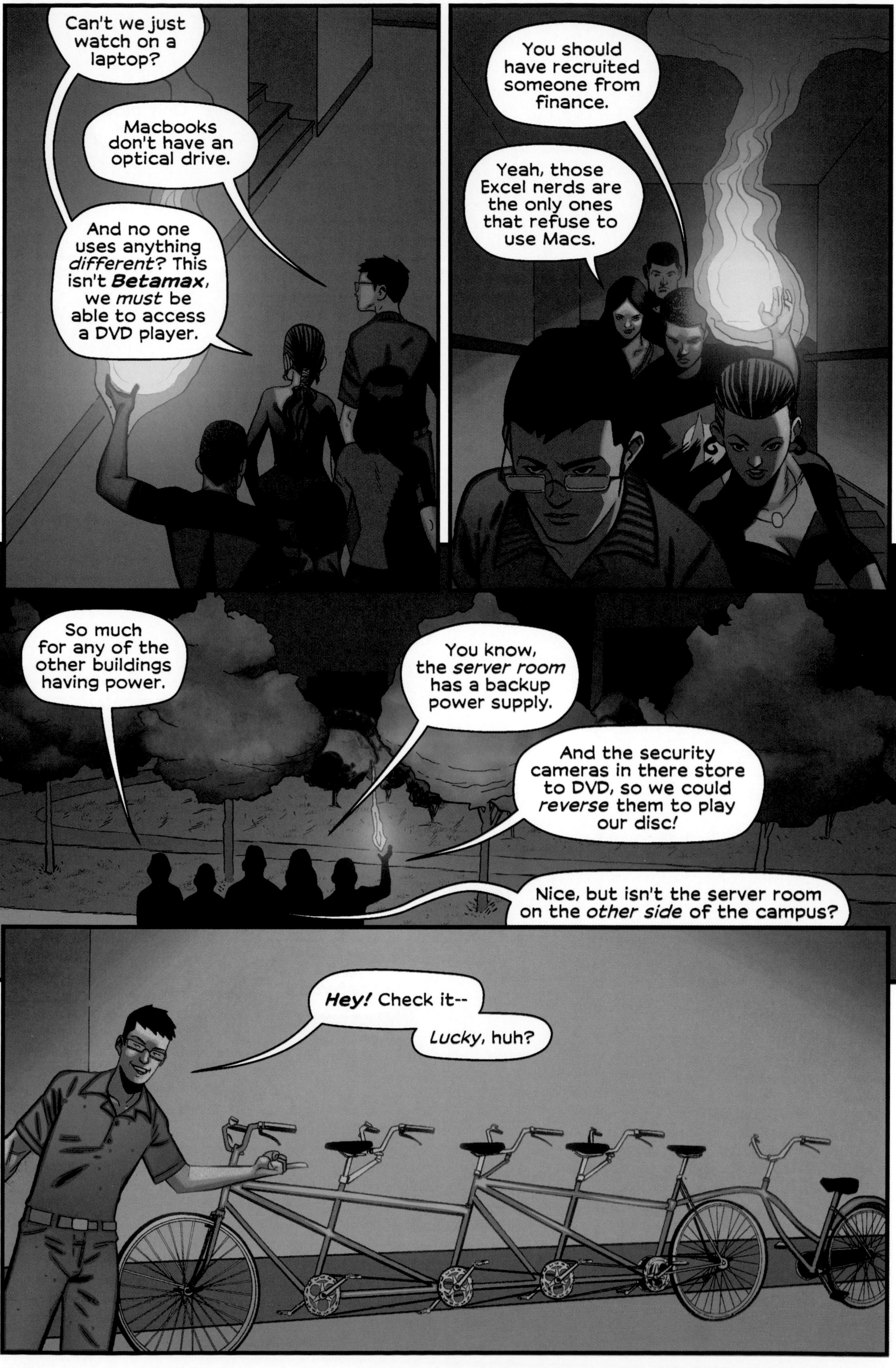
Can't we just watch on a laptop?
Macbooks don't have an optical drive.
And no one uses anything *different*? This isn't ***Betamax***, we *must* be able to access a DVD player.
You should have recruited someone from finance.
Yeah, those Excel nerds are the only ones that refuse to use Macs.
So much for any of the other buildings having power.
You know, the *server room* has a backup power supply.
And the security cameras in there store to DVD, so we could *reverse* them to play our disc!
Nice, but isn't the server room on the *other side* of the campus?
Hey! Check it--
Lucky, huh?

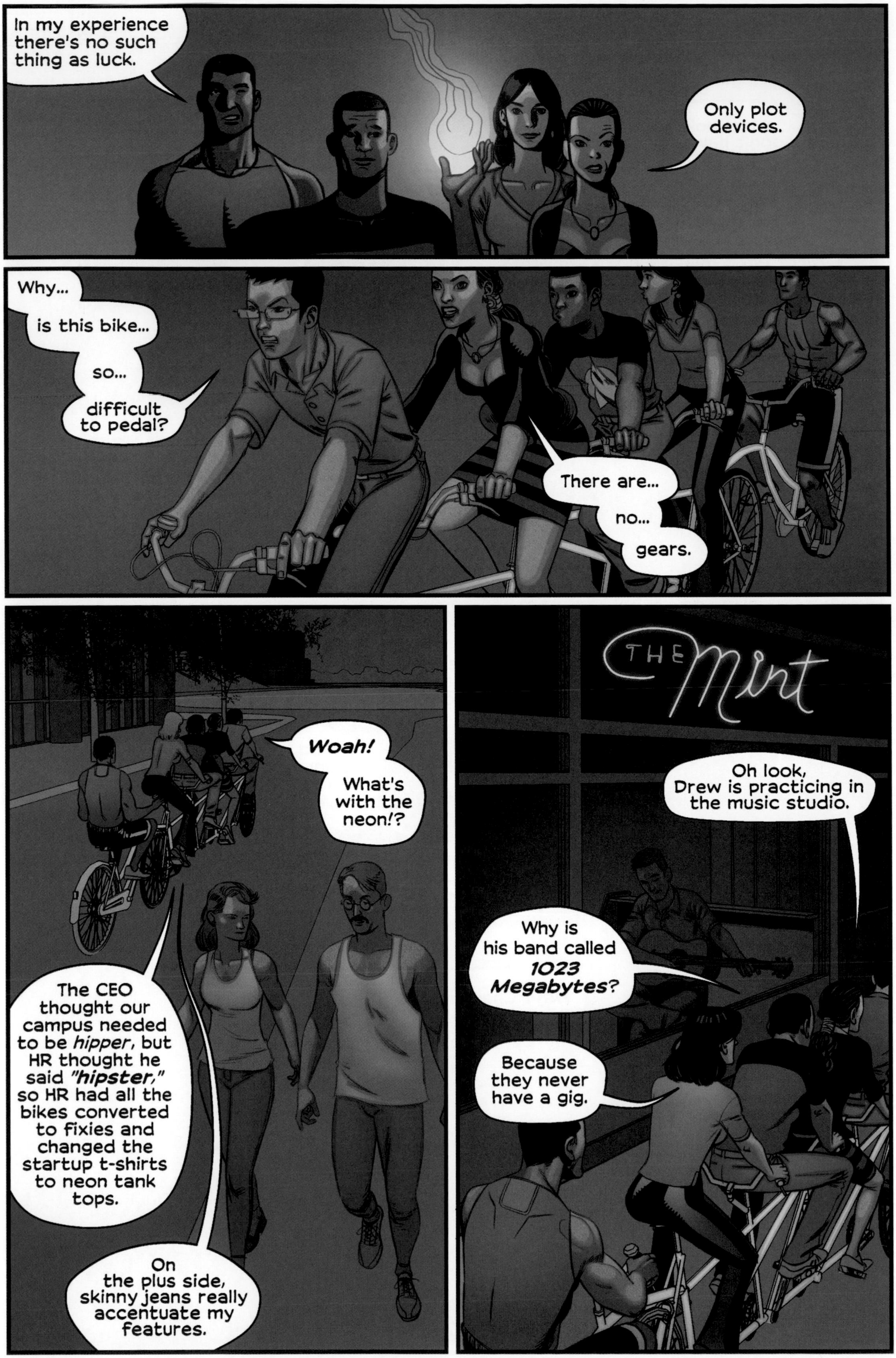
In my experience there's no such thing as luck.
Only plot devices.
Why...
is this bike...
so...
difficult to pedal?
There are...
no...
gears.
Woah!
What's with the neon!?
The CEO thought our campus needed to be *hipper*, but HR thought he said ***"hipster,"*** so HR had all the bikes converted to fixies and changed the startup t-shirts to neon tank tops.
On the plus side, skinny jeans really accentuate my features.
THE Mint
Oh look, Drew is practicing in the music studio.
Why is his band called ***1023 Megabytes***?
Because they never have a gig.

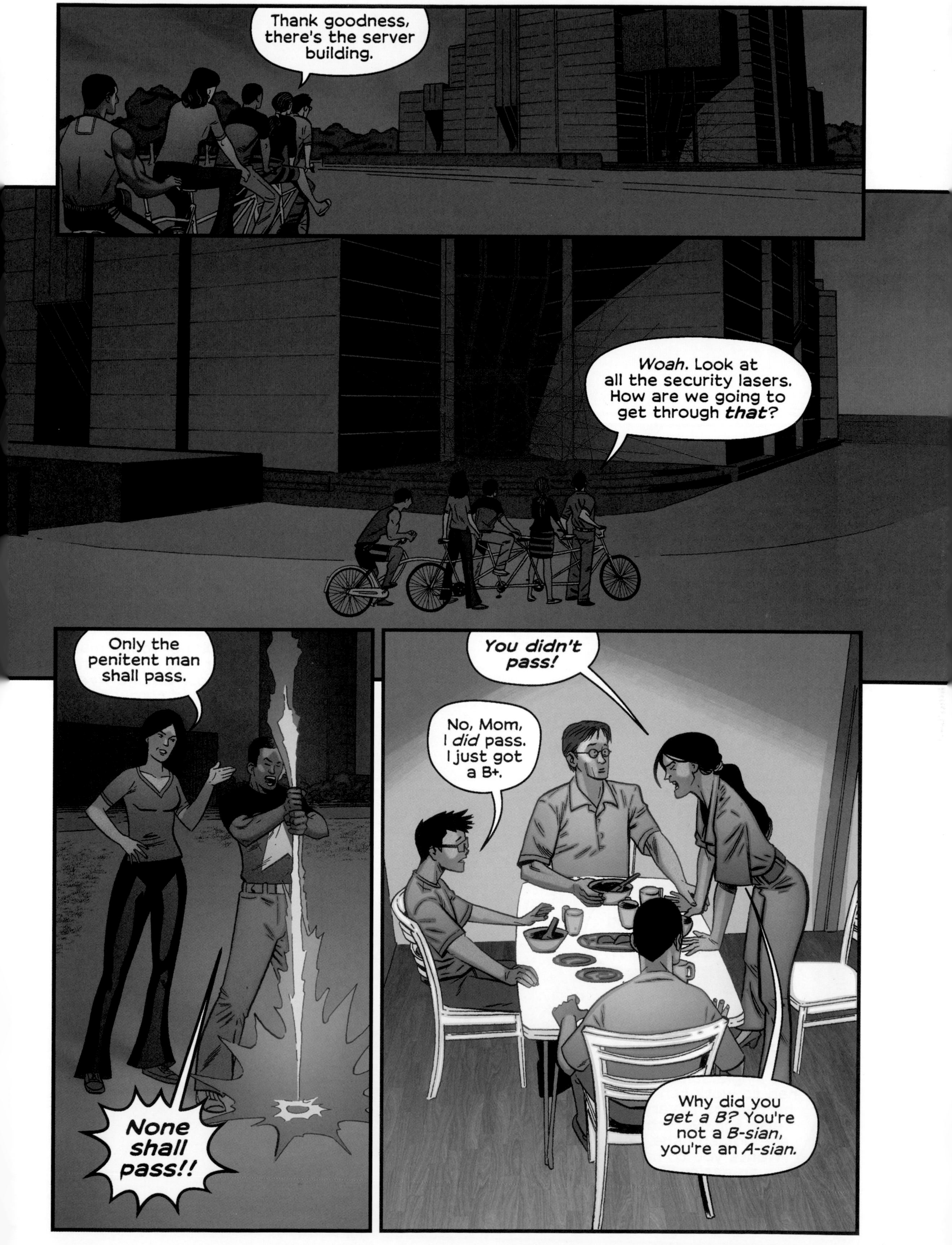
Thank goodness, there's the server building.
Woah. Look at all the security lasers. How are we going to get through ***that***?
Only the penitent man shall pass.
None shall pass!!
You didn't pass!
No, Mom, I *did* pass. I just got a B+.
Why did you *get a B?* You're not a *B-sian*, you're an *A-sian*.

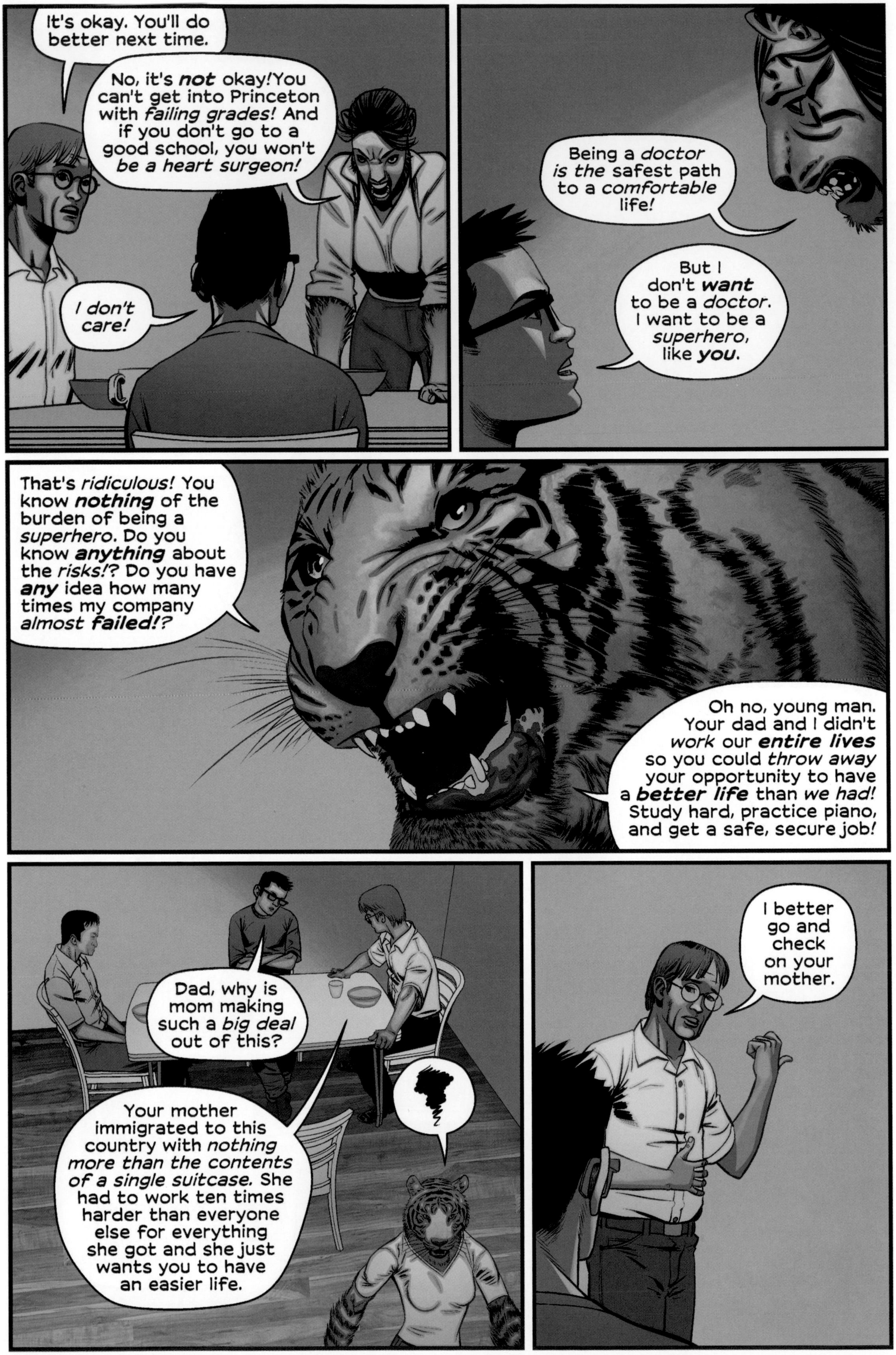
It's okay. You'll do better next time.
No, it's *not* okay! You can't get into Princeton with *failing grades!* And if you don't go to a good school, you won't *be a heart surgeon!*
I don't care!
Being a *doctor is the* safest path to a *comfortable* life!
But I don't ***want*** to be a *doctor*. I want to be a *superhero*, like ***you***.
That's *ridiculous!* You know ***nothing*** of the burden of being a *superhero*. Do you know ***anything*** about the *risks!?* Do you have ***any*** idea how many times my company *almost* ***failed!?***
Oh no, young man. Your dad and I didn't *work* our ***entire lives*** so you could *throw away* your opportunity to have a ***better life*** than *we had!* Study hard, practice piano, and get a safe, secure job!
Dad, why is mom making such a *big deal* out of this?
Your mother immigrated to this country with *nothing more than the contents of a single suitcase.* She had to work ten times harder than everyone else for everything she got and she just wants you to have an easier life.
I better go and check on your mother.

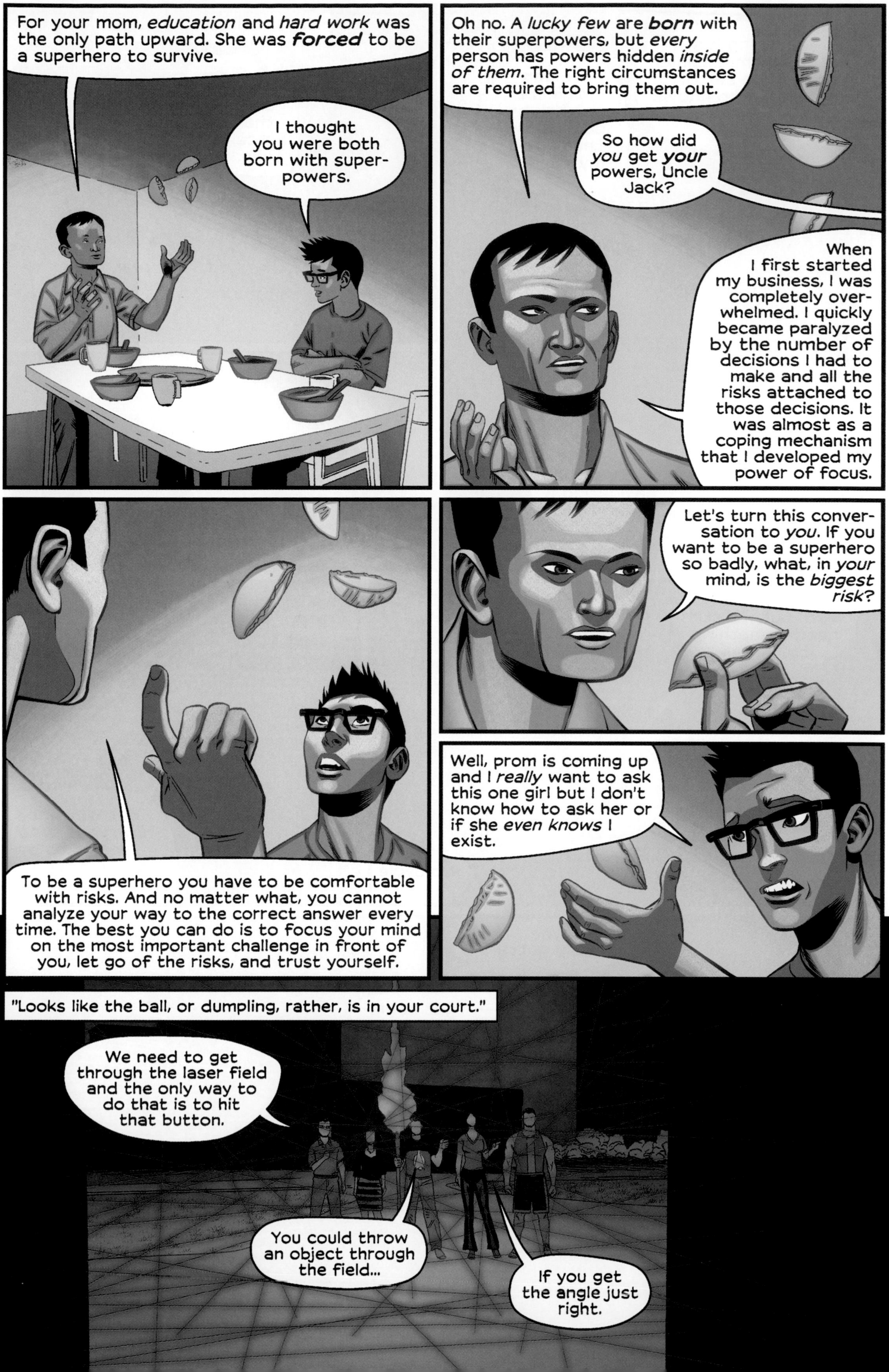
For your mom, *education* and *hard work* was the only path upward. She was ***forced*** to be a superhero to survive.
I thought you were both born with super-powers.
Oh no. A *lucky few* are ***born*** with their superpowers, but *every* person has powers hidden *inside of them*. The right circumstances are required to bring them out.
So how did *you* get ***your*** powers, Uncle Jack?
When I first started my business, I was completely over-whelmed. I quickly became paralyzed by the number of decisions I had to make and all the risks attached to those decisions. It was almost as a coping mechanism that I developed my power of focus.
To be a superhero you have to be comfortable with risks. And no matter what, you cannot analyze your way to the correct answer every time. The best you can do is to focus your mind on the most important challenge in front of you, let go of the risks, and trust yourself.
Let's turn this conver-sation to *you*. If you want to be a superhero so badly, what, in *your* mind, is the *biggest risk*?
Well, prom is coming up and I *really* want to ask this one girl but I don't know how to ask her or if she *even knows* I exist.
"Looks like the ball, or dumpling, rather, is in your court."
We need to get through the laser field and the only way to do that is to hit that button.
You could throw an object through the field...
If you get the angle just right.

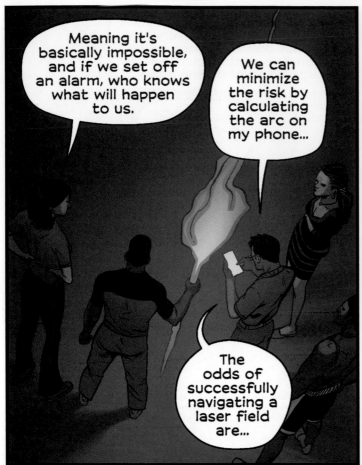

Meaning it's basically impossible, and if we set off an alarm, who knows what will happen to us.

We can minimize the risk by calculating the arc on my phone...

The odds of successfully navigating a laser field are...

Never tell me the odds.

But--

Use the Force, Luke.

Yeah yeah, but this isn't the movies.

Let go, Luke.

Trust your *feelings*.

Alright already, Ben, but we still need something to throw.

A bicycle seat?

This is crazy...

But why not? *Everyone else* seems to be getting super-powers tonight.

And Jayne, you've really gotta--

--huff--

get some new movies to quote.

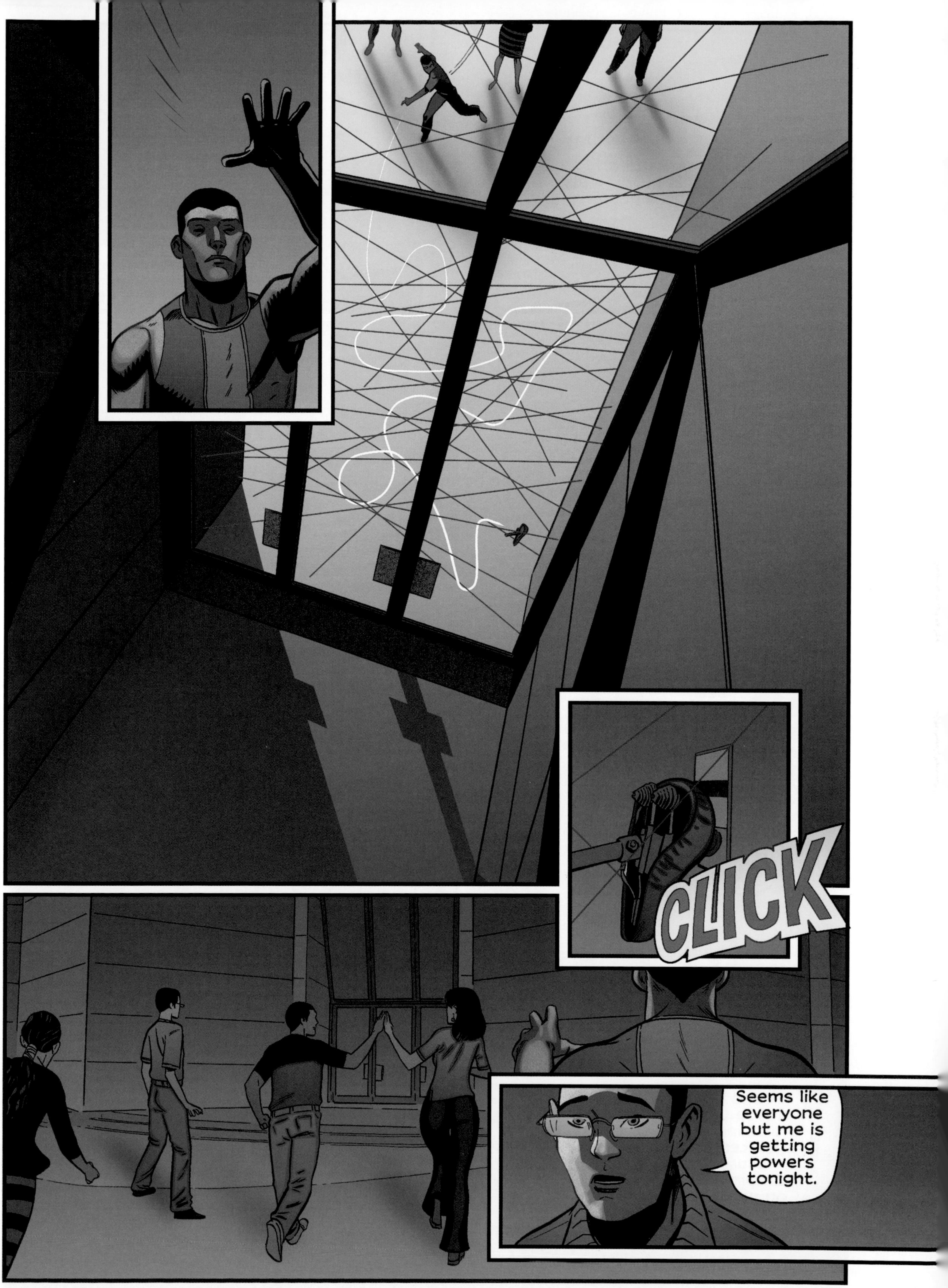
CLICK
Seems like everyone but me is getting powers tonight.

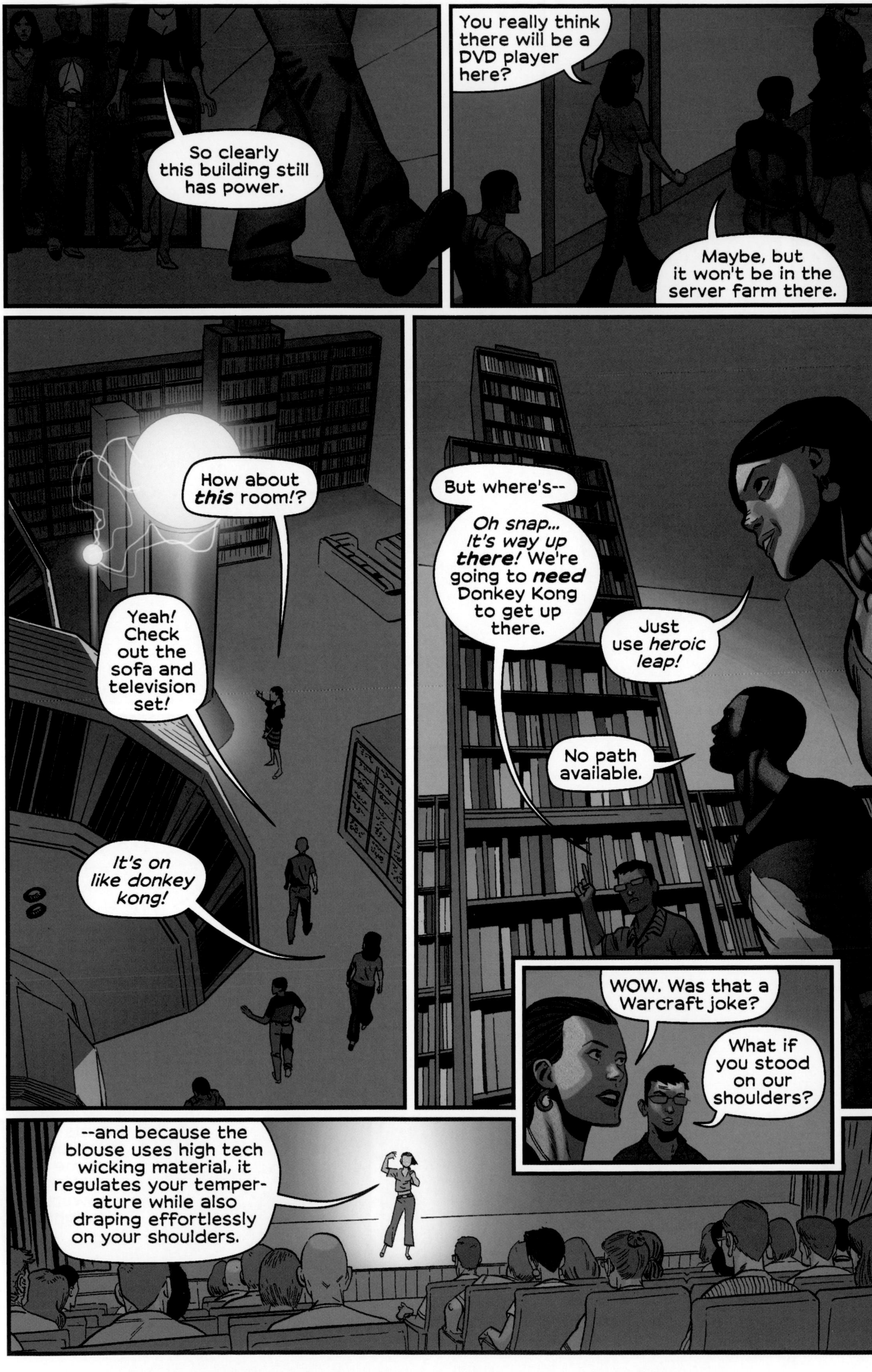
So clearly this building still has power.
You really think there will be a DVD player here?
Maybe, but it won't be in the server farm there.
How about *this* room!?
Yeah! Check out the sofa and television set!
It's on like donkey kong!
But where's--
Oh snap... It's way up ***there!*** We're going to ***need*** Donkey Kong to get up there.
Just use *heroic leap!*
No path available.
WOW. Was that a Warcraft joke?
What if you stood on our shoulders?
--and because the blouse uses high tech wicking material, it regulates your temper-ature while also draping effortlessly on your shoulders.

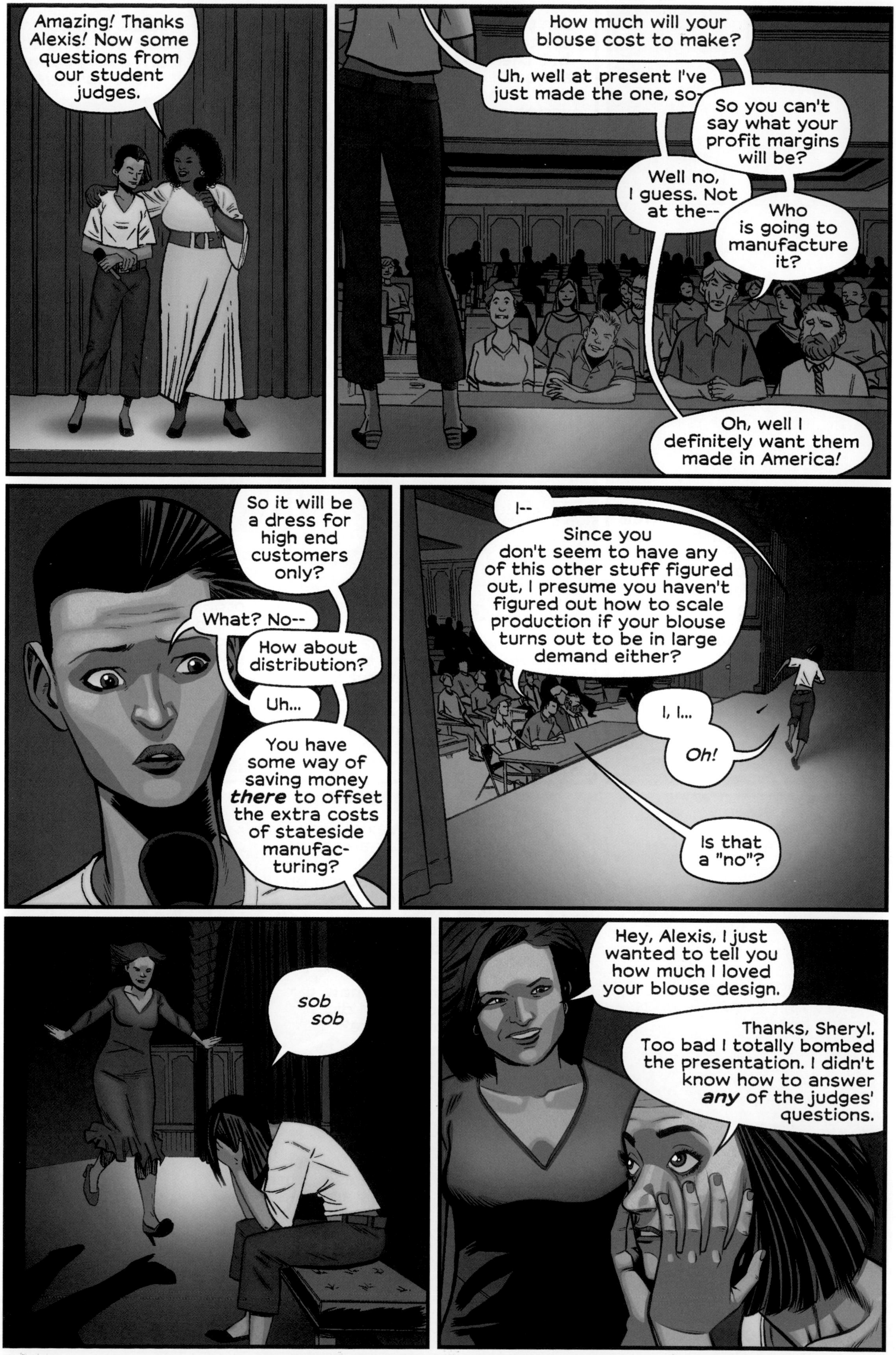

Amazing! Thanks Alexis! Now some questions from our student judges.
How much will your blouse cost to make?
Uh, well at present I've just made the one, so-
So you can't say what your profit margins will be?
Well no, I guess. Not at the--
Who is going to manufacture it?
Oh, well I definitely want them made in America!
So it will be a dress for high end customers only?
What? No--
How about distribution?
Uh...
You have some way of saving money *there* to offset the extra costs of stateside manufac-turing?
I--
Since you don't seem to have any of this other stuff figured out, I presume you haven't figured out how to scale production if your blouse turns out to be in large demand either?
I, I...
Oh!
Is that a "no"?
sob sob
Hey, Alexis, I just wanted to tell you how much I loved your blouse design.
Thanks, Sheryl. Too bad I totally bombed the presentation. I didn't know how to answer *any* of the judges' questions.

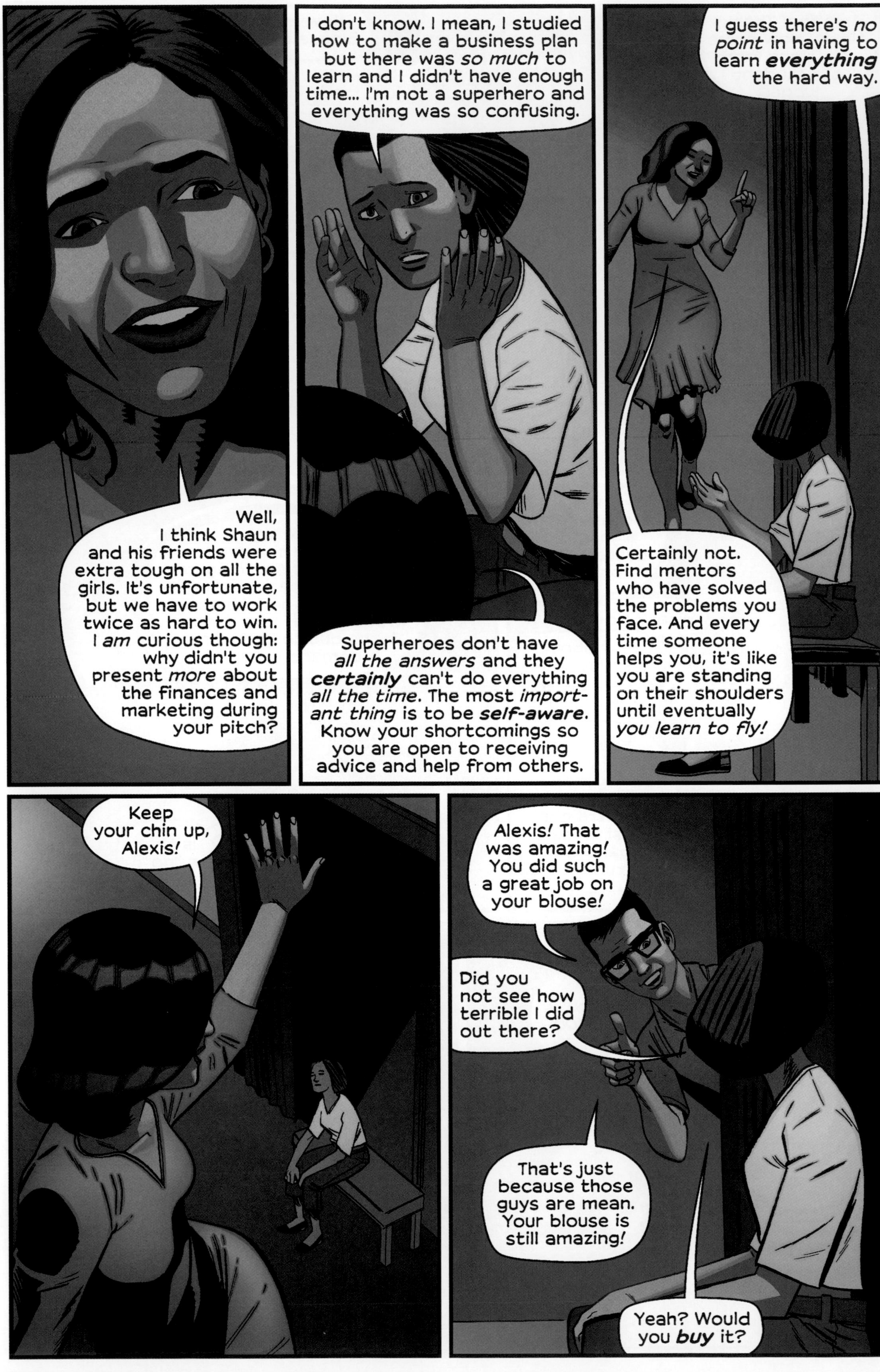
Well, I think Shaun and his friends were extra tough on all the girls. It's unfortunate, but we have to work twice as hard to win. I *am* curious though: why didn't you present *more* about the finances and marketing during your pitch?
I don't know. I mean, I studied how to make a business plan but there was *so much* to learn and I didn't have enough time... I'm not a superhero and everything was so confusing.
Superheroes don't have *all the answers* and they ***certainly*** can't do everything *all the time*. The most *important thing* is to be ***self-aware***. Know your shortcomings so you are open to receiving advice and help from others.
I guess there's *no point* in having to learn ***everything*** the hard way.
Certainly not. Find mentors who have solved the problems you face. And every time someone helps you, it's like you are standing on their shoulders until eventually *you learn to fly!*
Keep your chin up, Alexis!
Alexis! That was amazing! You did such a great job on your blouse!
Did you not see how terrible I did out there?
That's just because those guys are mean. Your blouse is still amazing!
Yeah? Would you ***buy*** it?

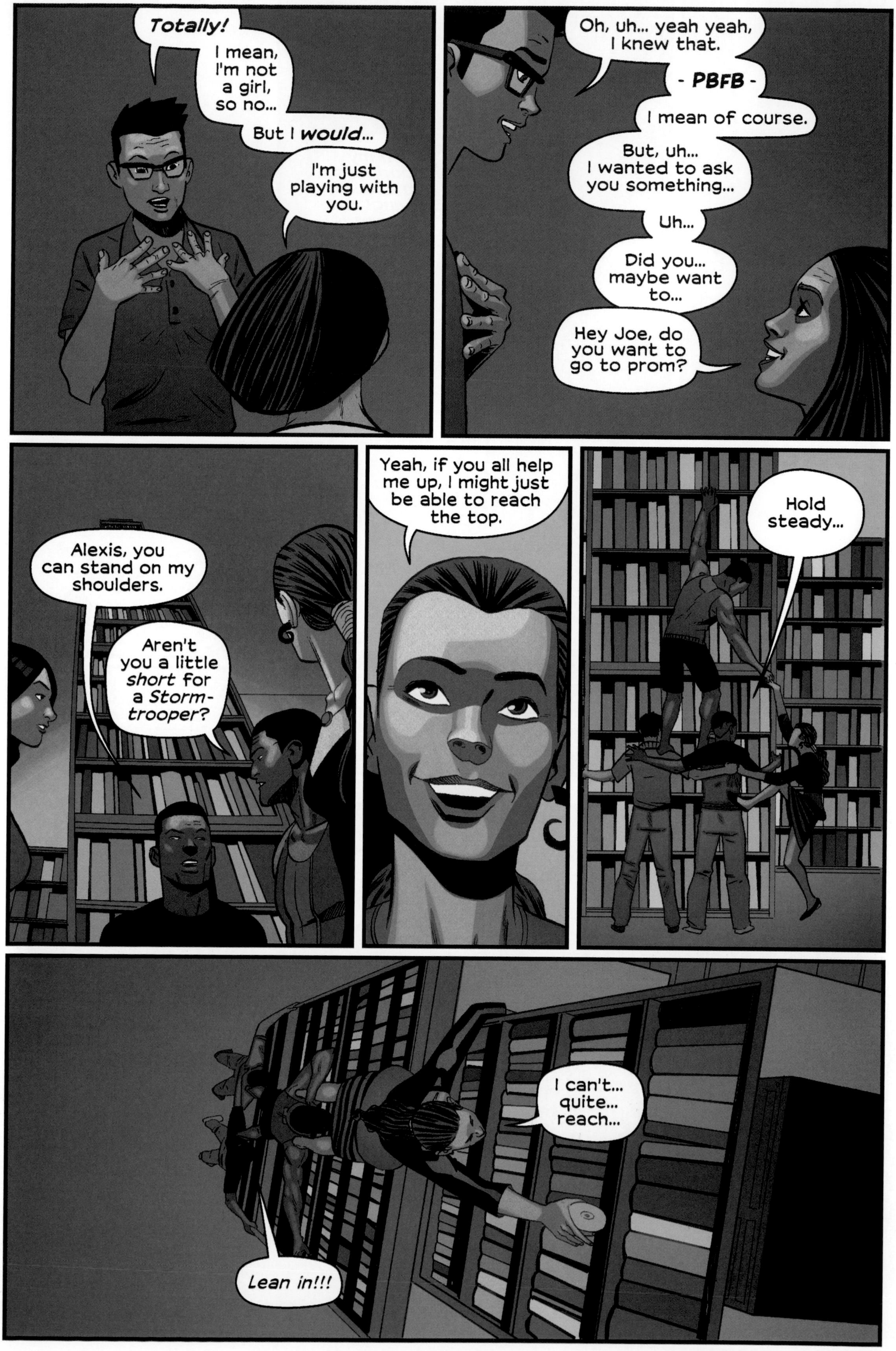

Totally!
I mean, I'm not a girl, so no...
But I ***would***...
I'm just playing with you.
Oh, uh... yeah yeah, I knew that.
- PBFB -
I mean of course.
But, uh... I wanted to ask you something...
Uh...
Did you... maybe want to...
Hey Joe, do you want to go to prom?
Alexis, you can stand on my shoulders.
Aren't you a little *short* for a *Storm-trooper*?
Yeah, if you all help me up, I might just be able to reach the top.
Hold steady...
I can't... quite... reach...
Lean in!!!

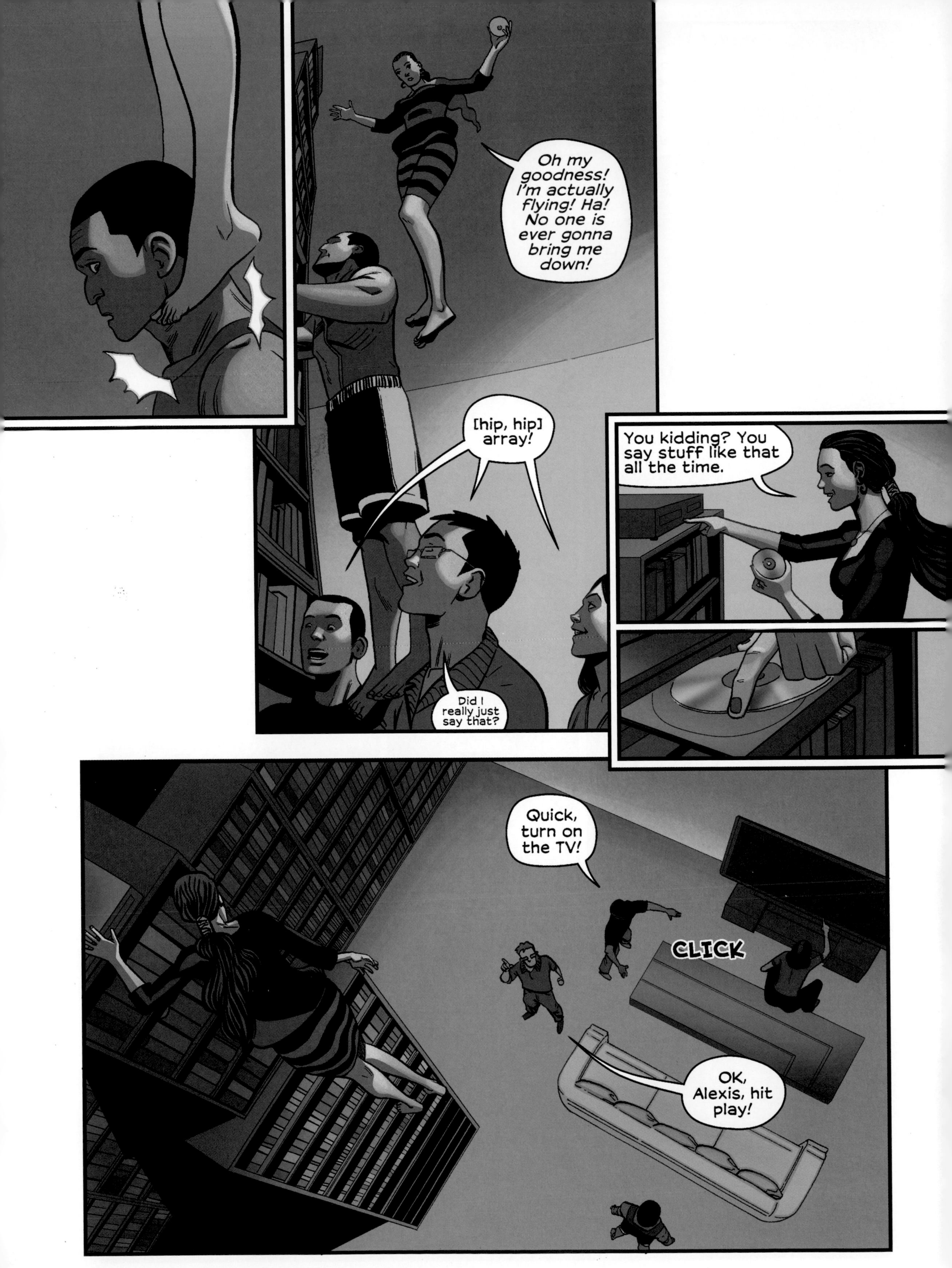

Oh my goodness! I'm actually flying! Ha! No one is ever gonna bring me down!
[hip, hip] array!
Did I really just say that?
You kidding? You say stuff like that all the time.
Quick, turn on the TV!
CLICK
OK, Alexis, hit play!

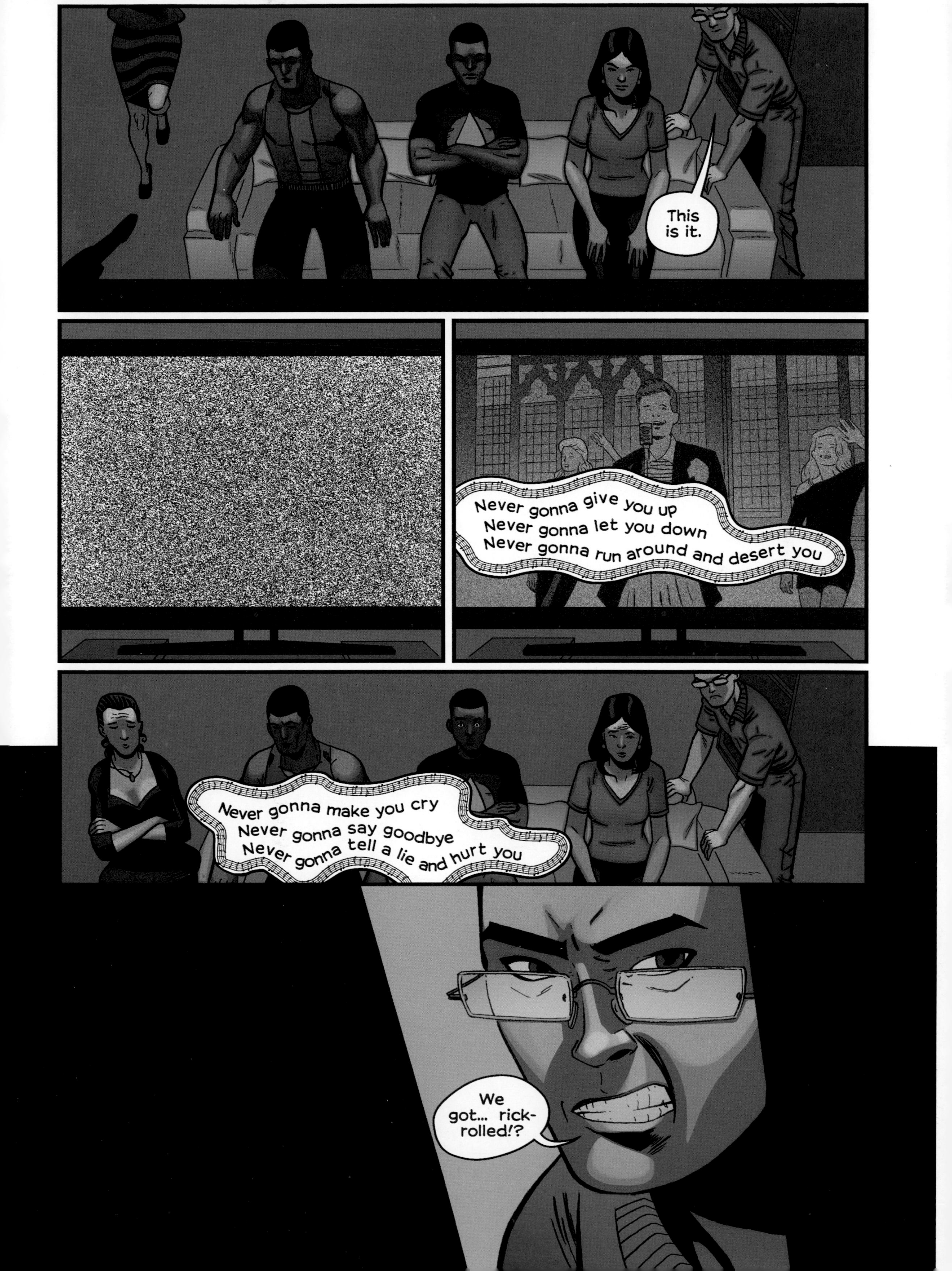
This is it.
Never gonna give you up
Never gonna let you down
Never gonna run around and desert you
Never gonna make you cry
Never gonna say goodbye
Never gonna tell a lie and hurt you
We got... rick-rolled!?

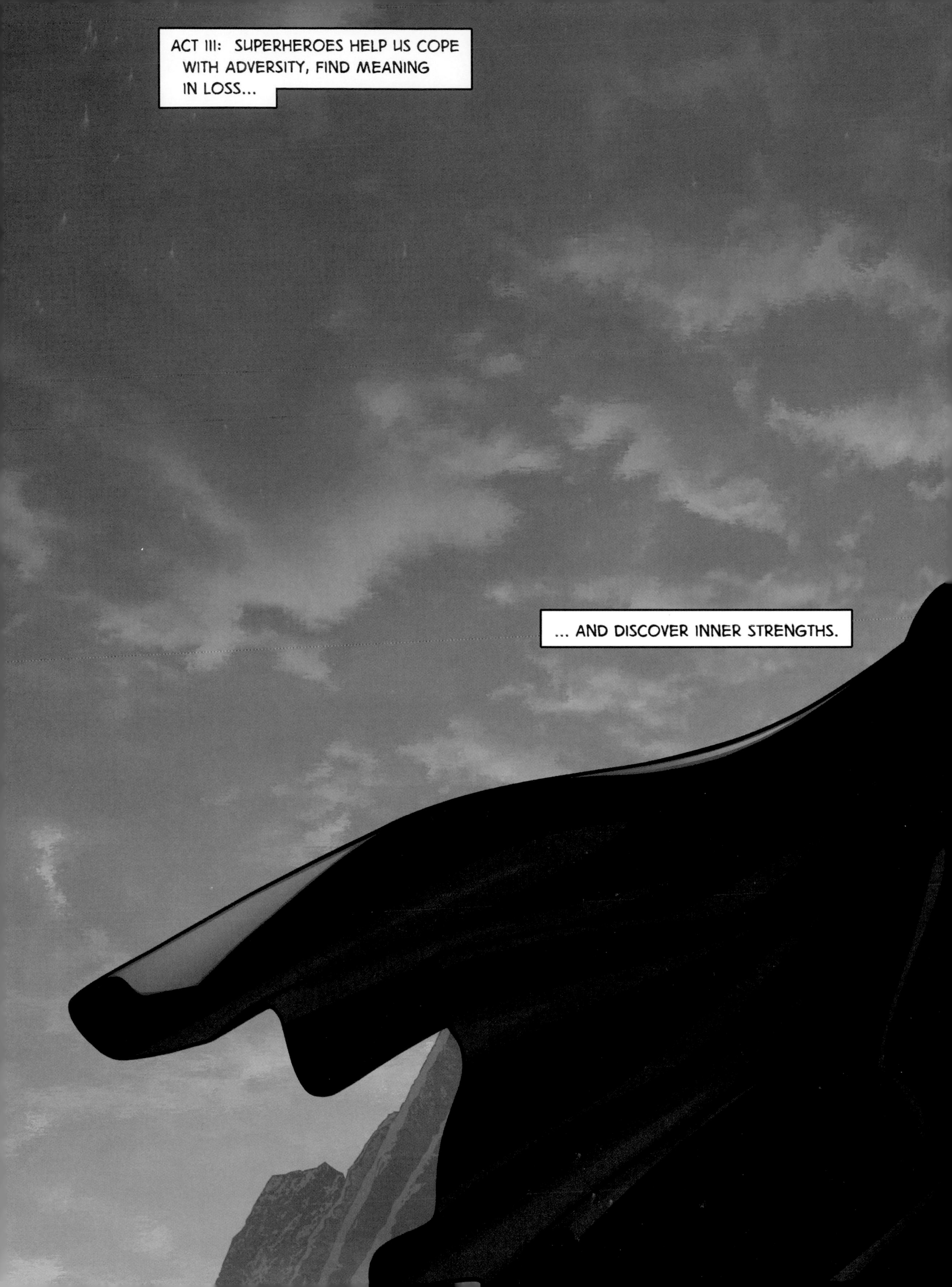
ACT III: SUPERHEROES HELP US COPE WITH ADVERSITY, FIND MEANING IN LOSS...
... AND DISCOVER INNER STRENGTHS.

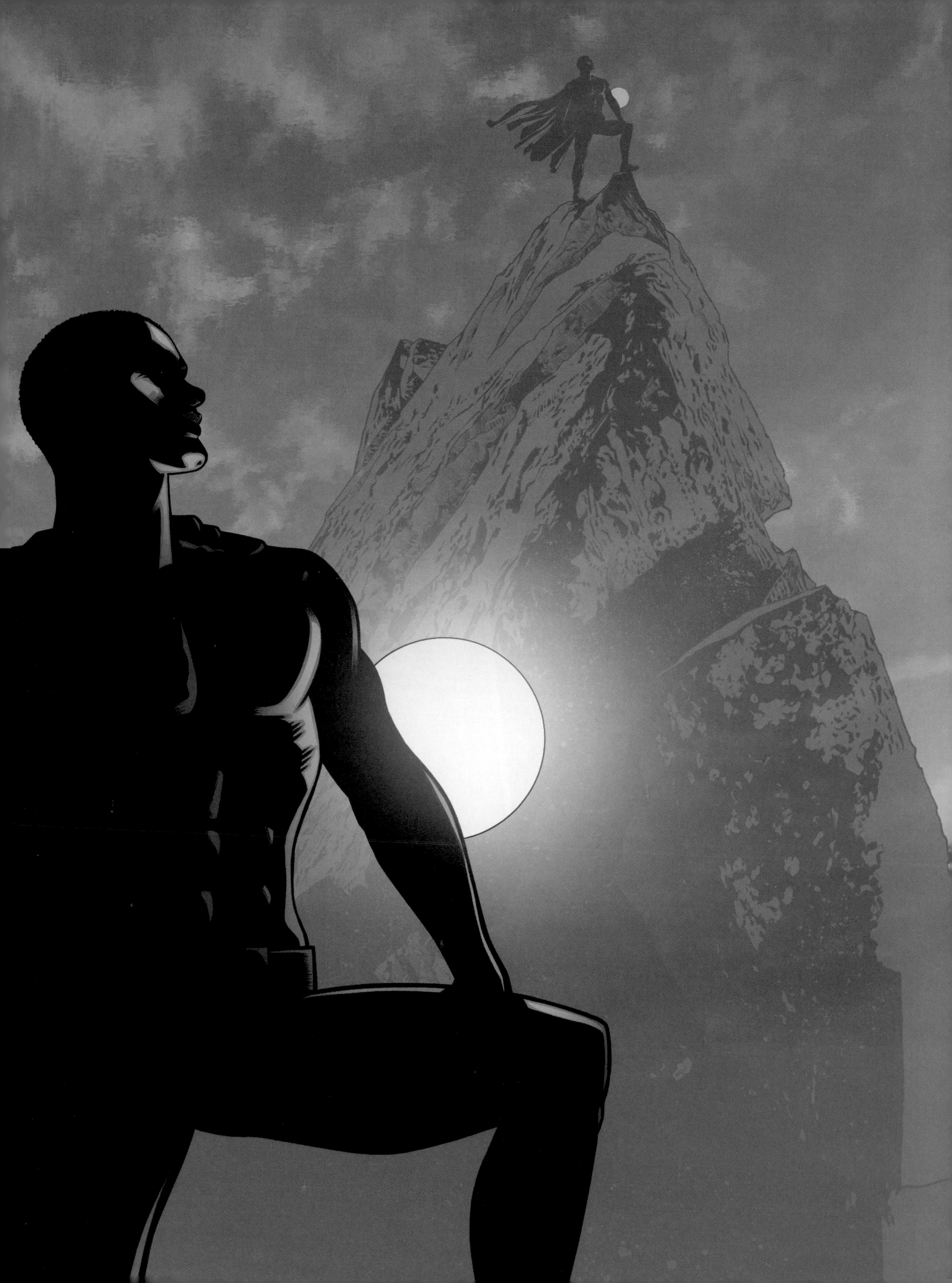

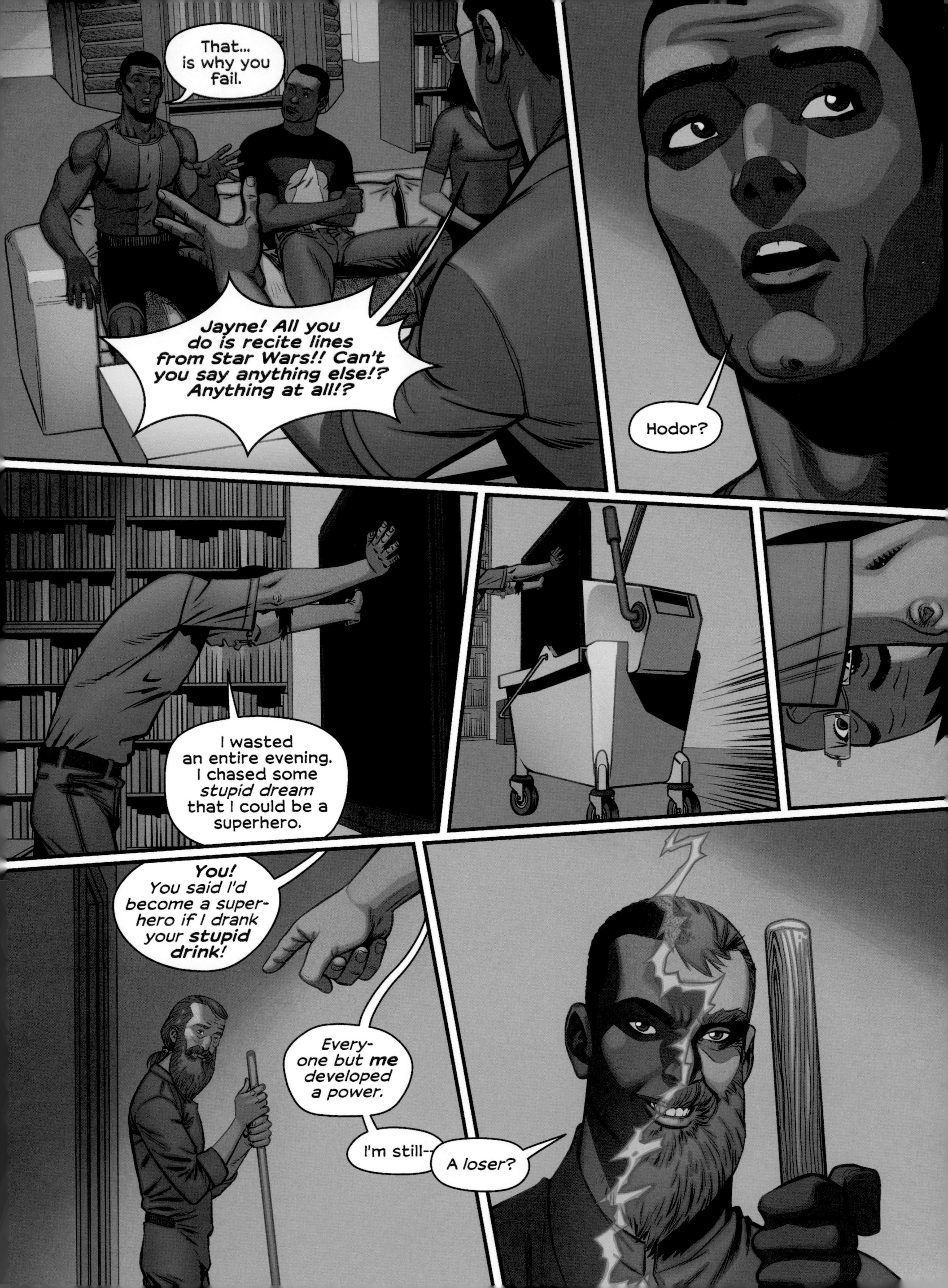
That... is why you fail.
Jayne! All you do is recite lines from Star Wars!! Can't you say anything else!? Anything at all!?
Hodor?
I wasted an entire evening. I chased some stupid dream that I could be a superhero.
You! You said I'd become a super-hero if I drank your stupid drink!
Every-one but me developed a power.
I'm still--
A loser?

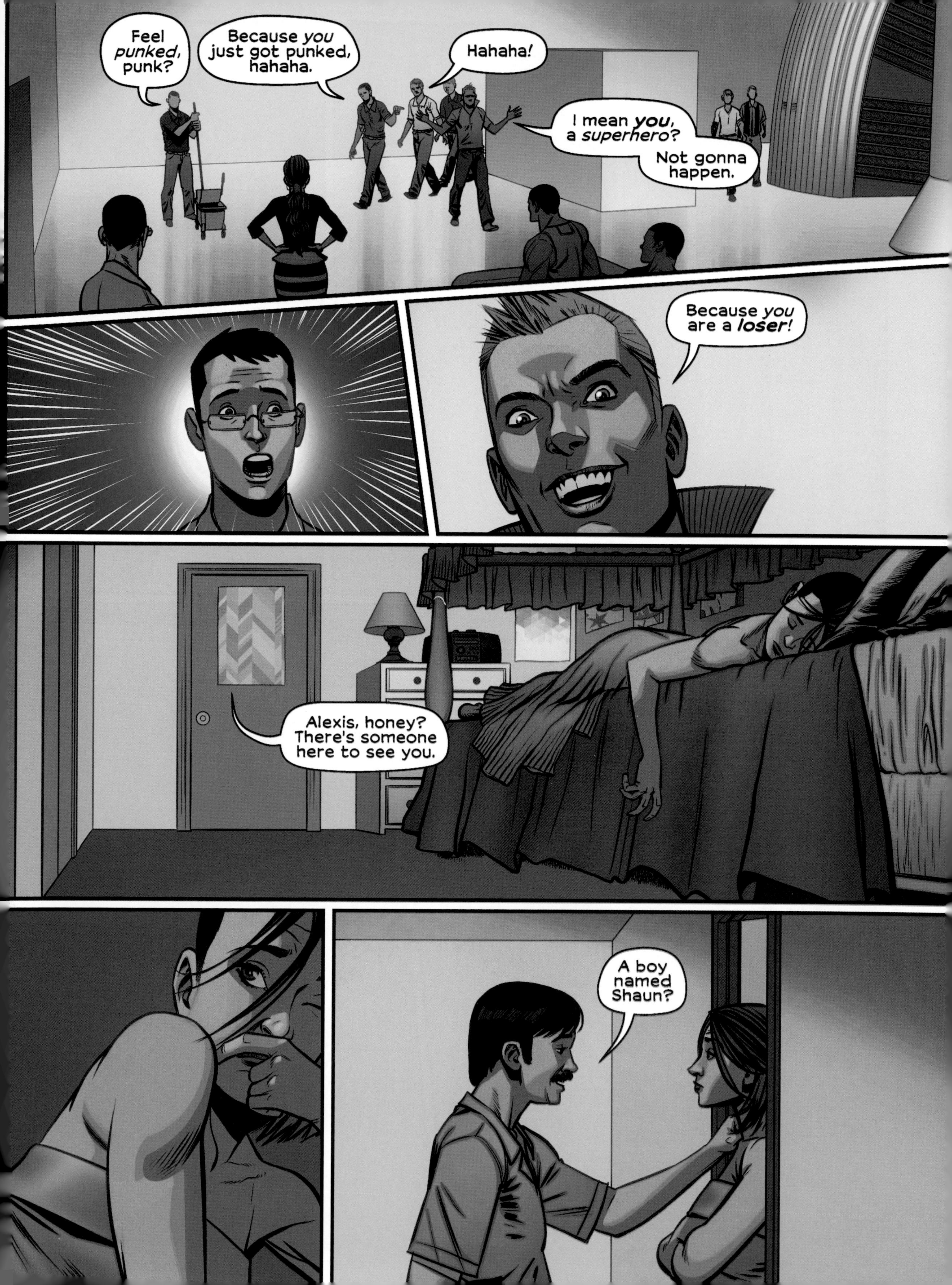
Feel *punked*, punk?
Because *you* just got punked, hahaha.
Hahaha!
I mean ***you***, a *superhero*?
Not gonna happen.
Because *you* are a ***loser***!
Alexis, honey? There's someone here to see you.
A boy named Shaun?

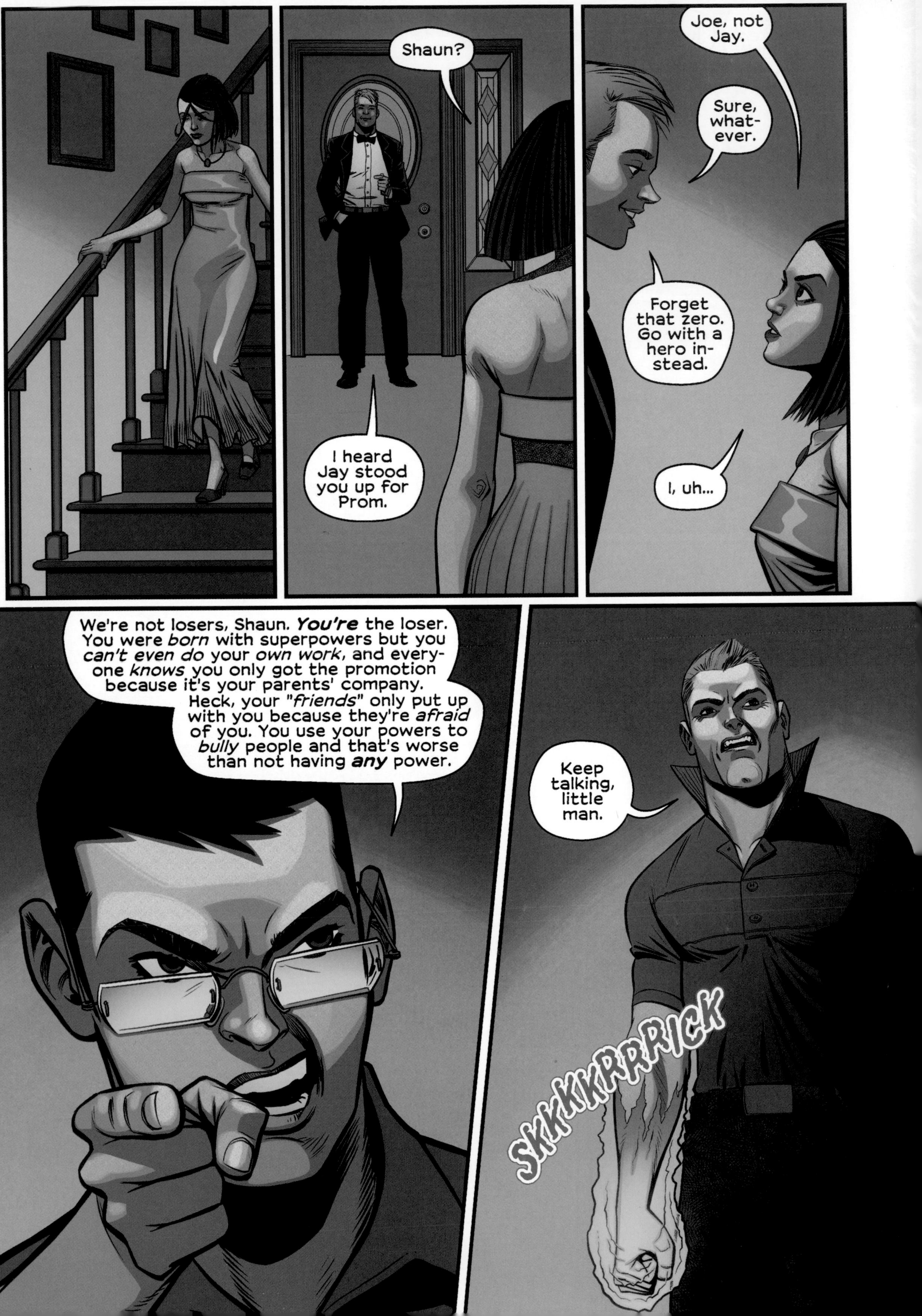

Shaun?
I heard Jay stood you up for Prom.
Joe, not Jay.
Sure, what-ever.
Forget that zero. Go with a hero in-stead.
I, uh...
We're not losers, Shaun. *You're* the loser. You were *born* with superpowers but you *can't even do* your *own work*, and every-one *knows* you only got the promotion because it's your parents' company. Heck, your "*friends*" only put up with you because they're *afraid* of you. You use your powers to *bully* people and that's worse than not having *any* power.
Keep talking, little man.
SKKKKRRRICK

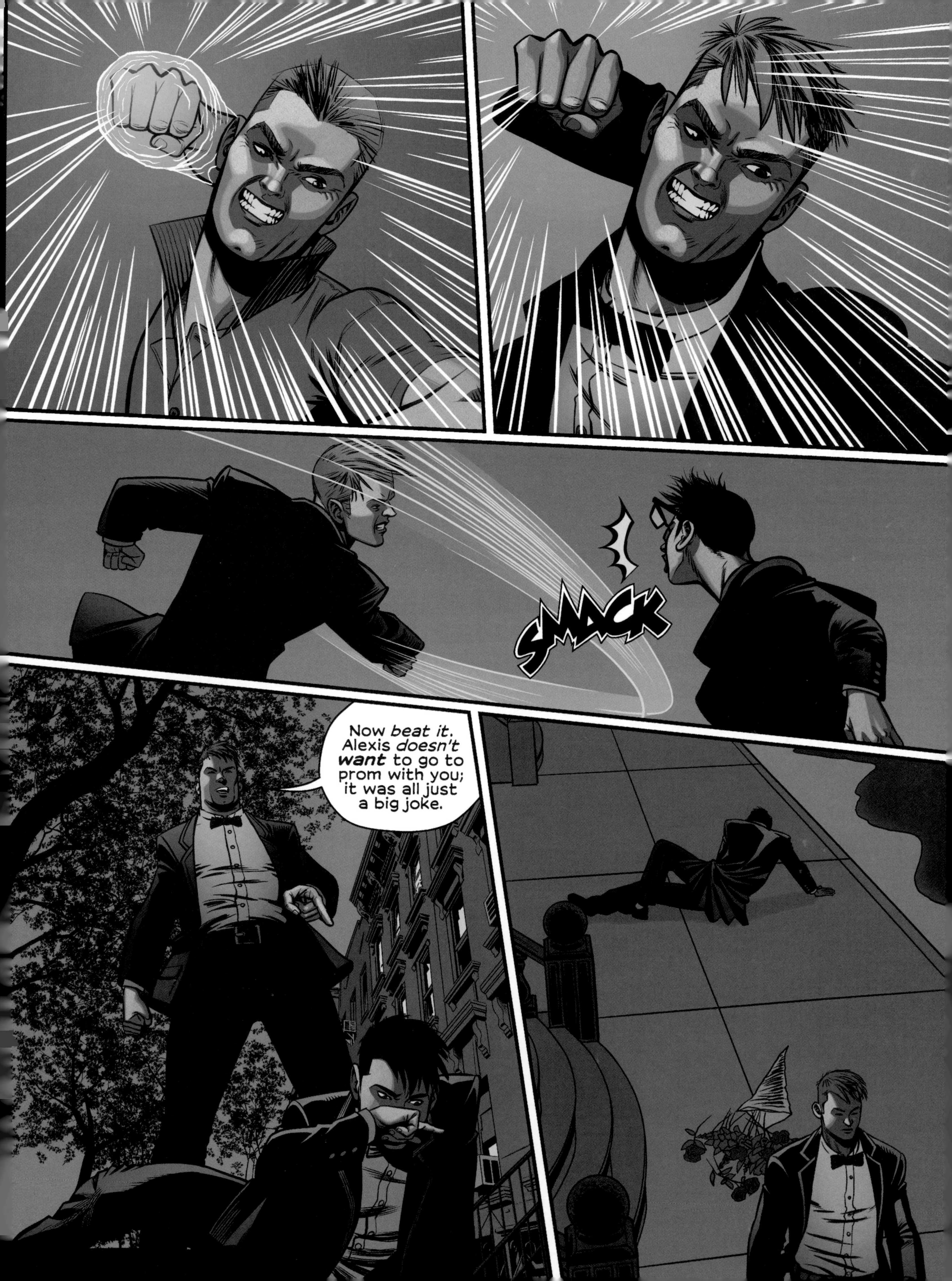
SMACK
Now *beat it*. Alexis *doesn't* ***want*** to go to prom with you; it was all just a big joke.

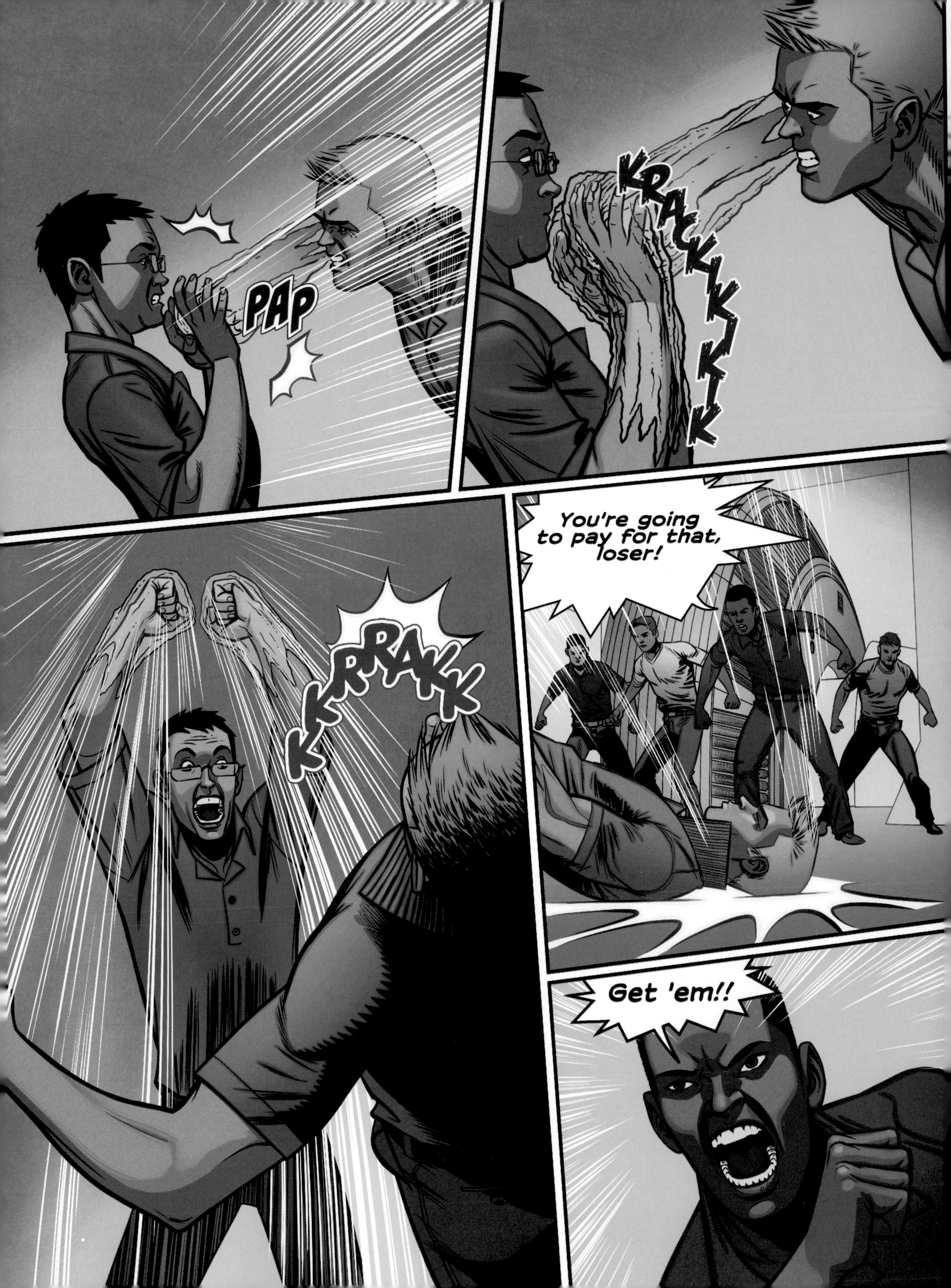
PAP
KRACKKKKK
KKRRRAKK
You're going to pay for that, loser!
Get 'em!!

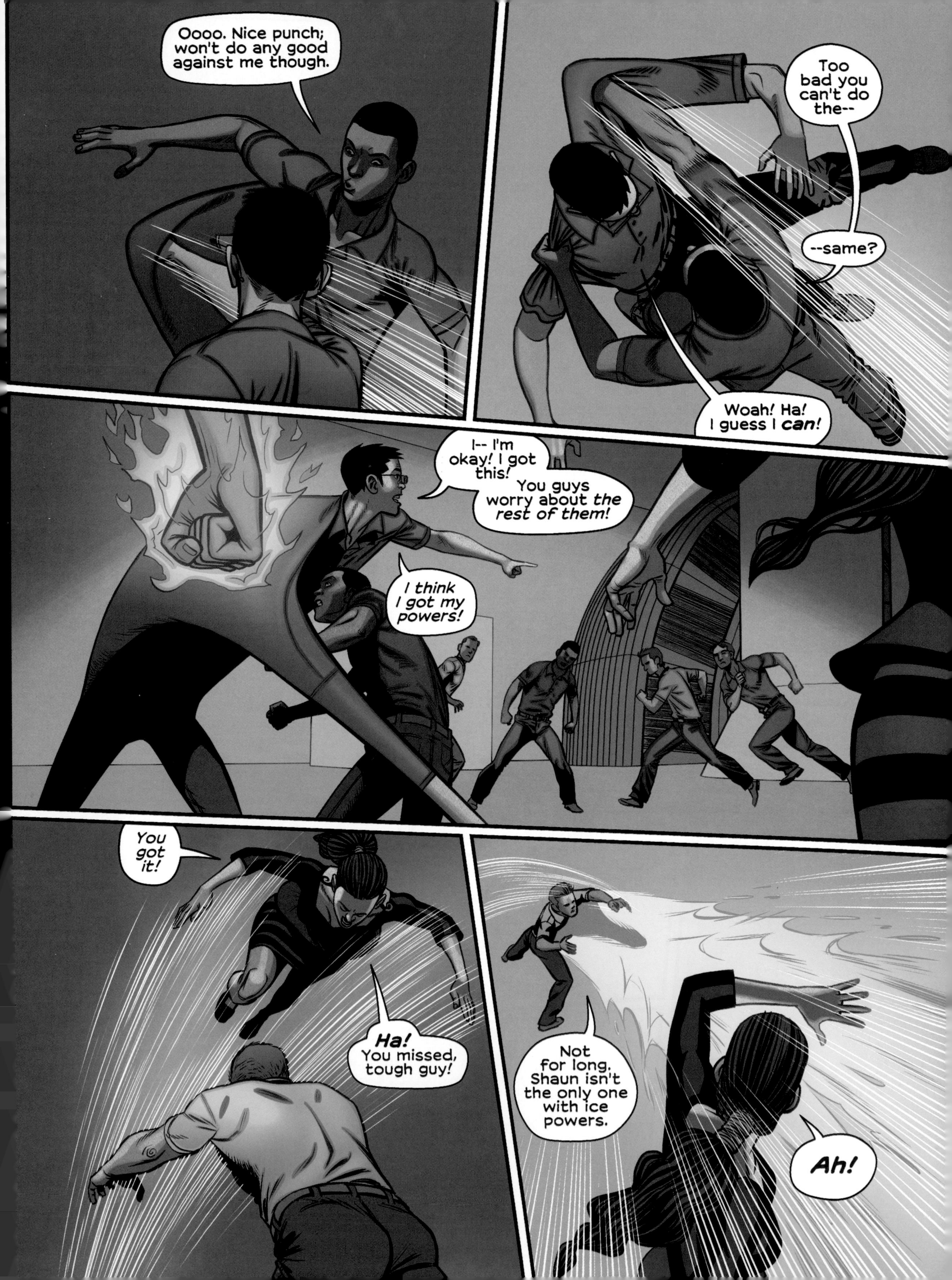
Oooo. Nice punch; won't do any good against me though.
Too bad you can't do the--
--same?
Woah! Ha! I guess I *can*!
I-- I'm okay! I got this!
You guys worry about *the rest of them!*
I think I got my powers!
You got it!
Ha! You missed, tough guy!
Not for long. Shaun isn't the only one with ice powers.
Ah!

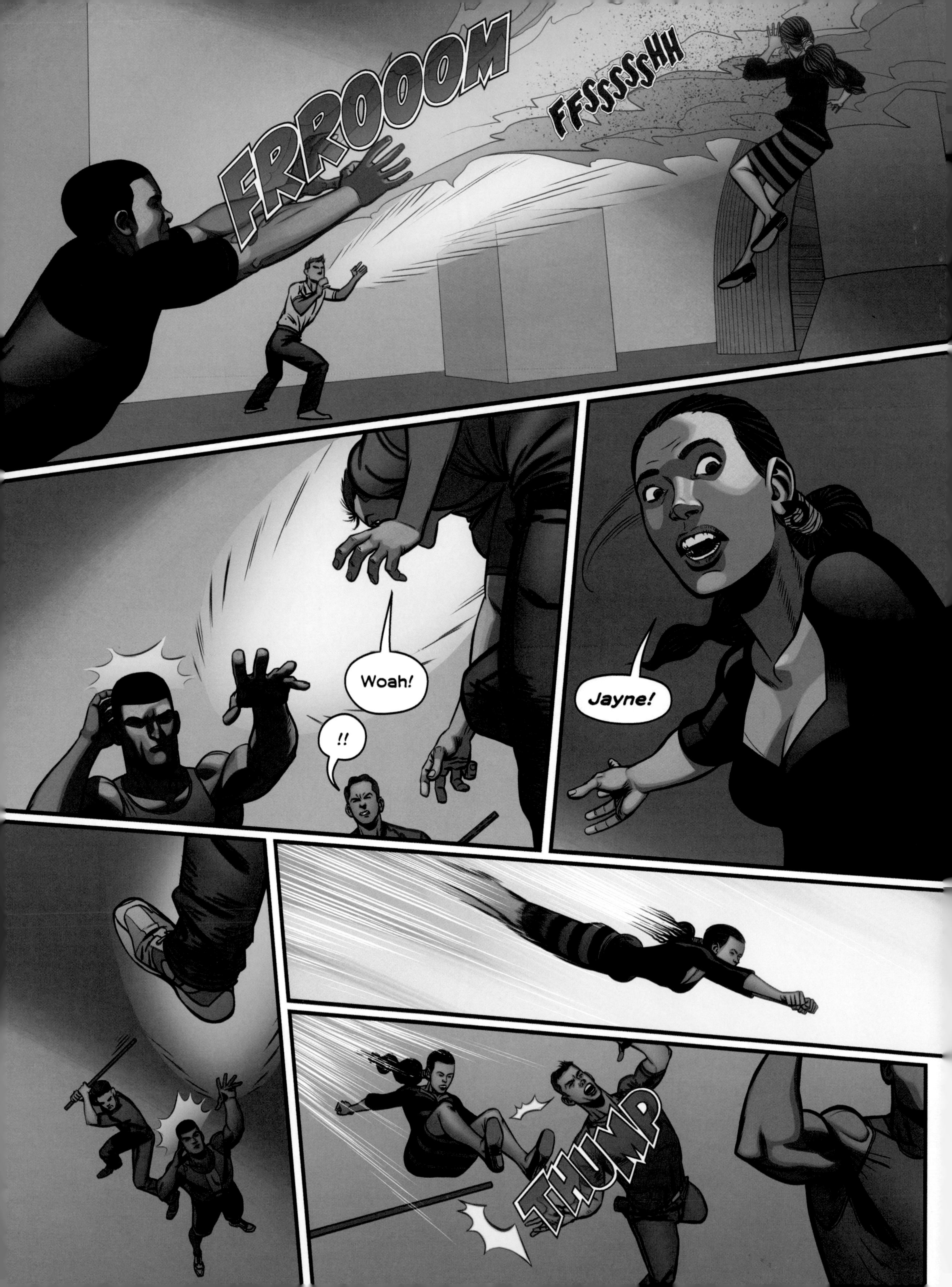
FRROOOM
FFSSSSSHH
Woah!
!!
Jayne!
THUMP

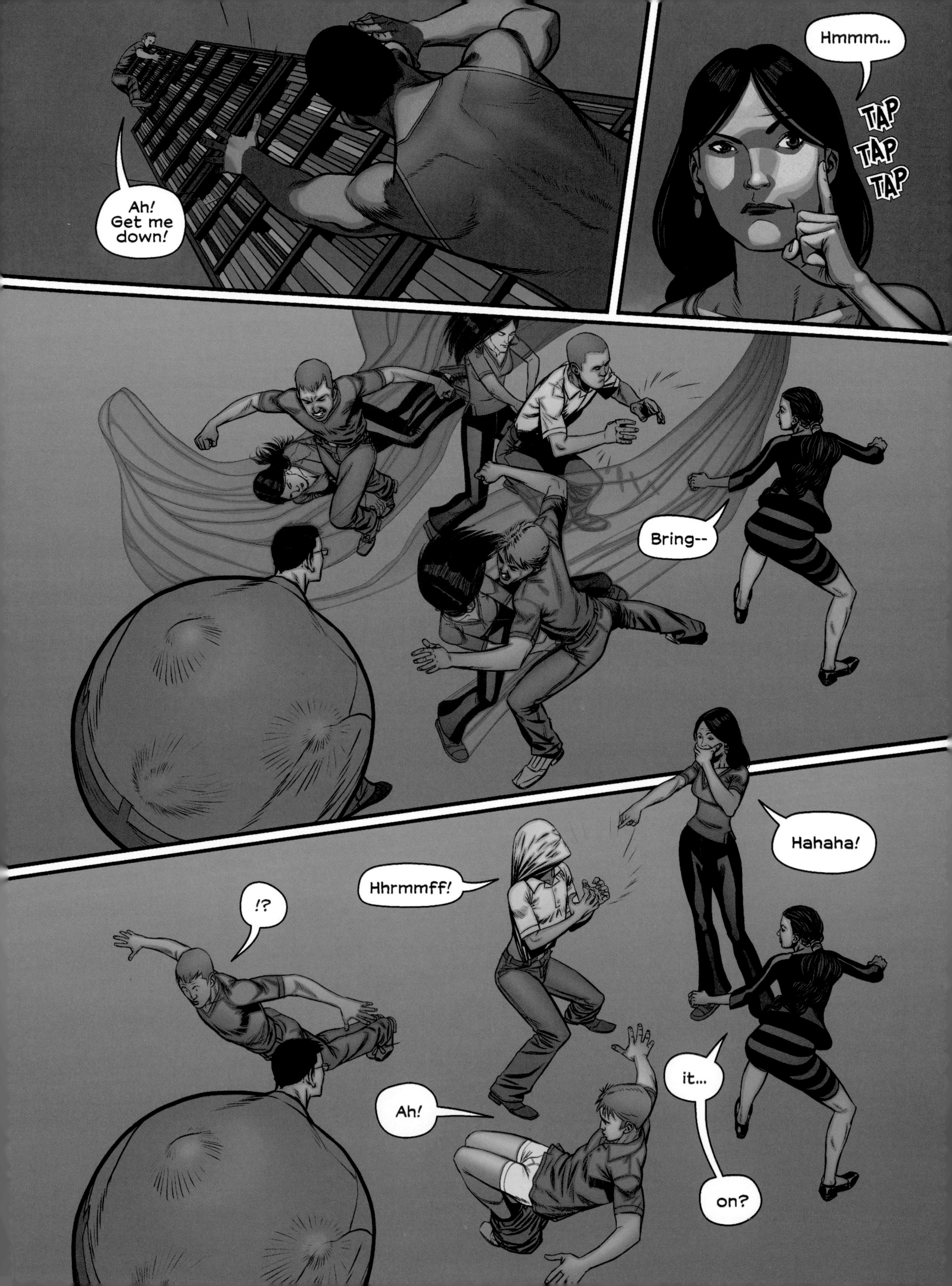
Ah! Get me down!
Hmmm...
TAP
TAP
TAP
Bring--
Hahaha!
Hhrmmff!
!?
it...
Ah!
on?

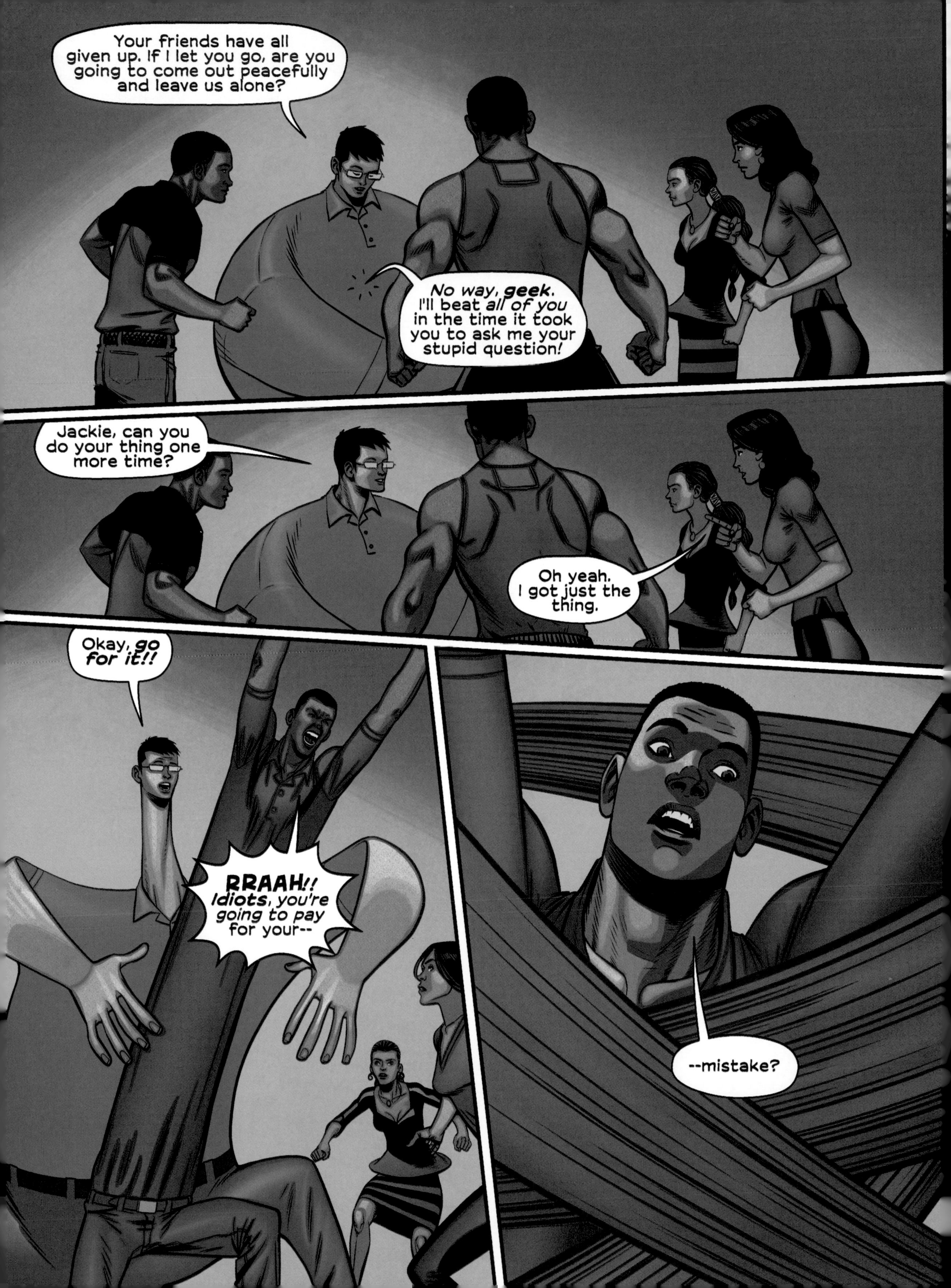
Your friends have all given up. If I let you go, are you going to come out peacefully and leave us alone?
*No way, **geek**.* I'll beat *all of you* in the time it took you to ask me your stupid question*!*
Jackie, can you do your thing one more time?
Oh yeah. I got just the thing.
Okay, ***go for it!!***
RRAAH*!!* ***Idiots**, you're going to pay for your--*
--mistake?

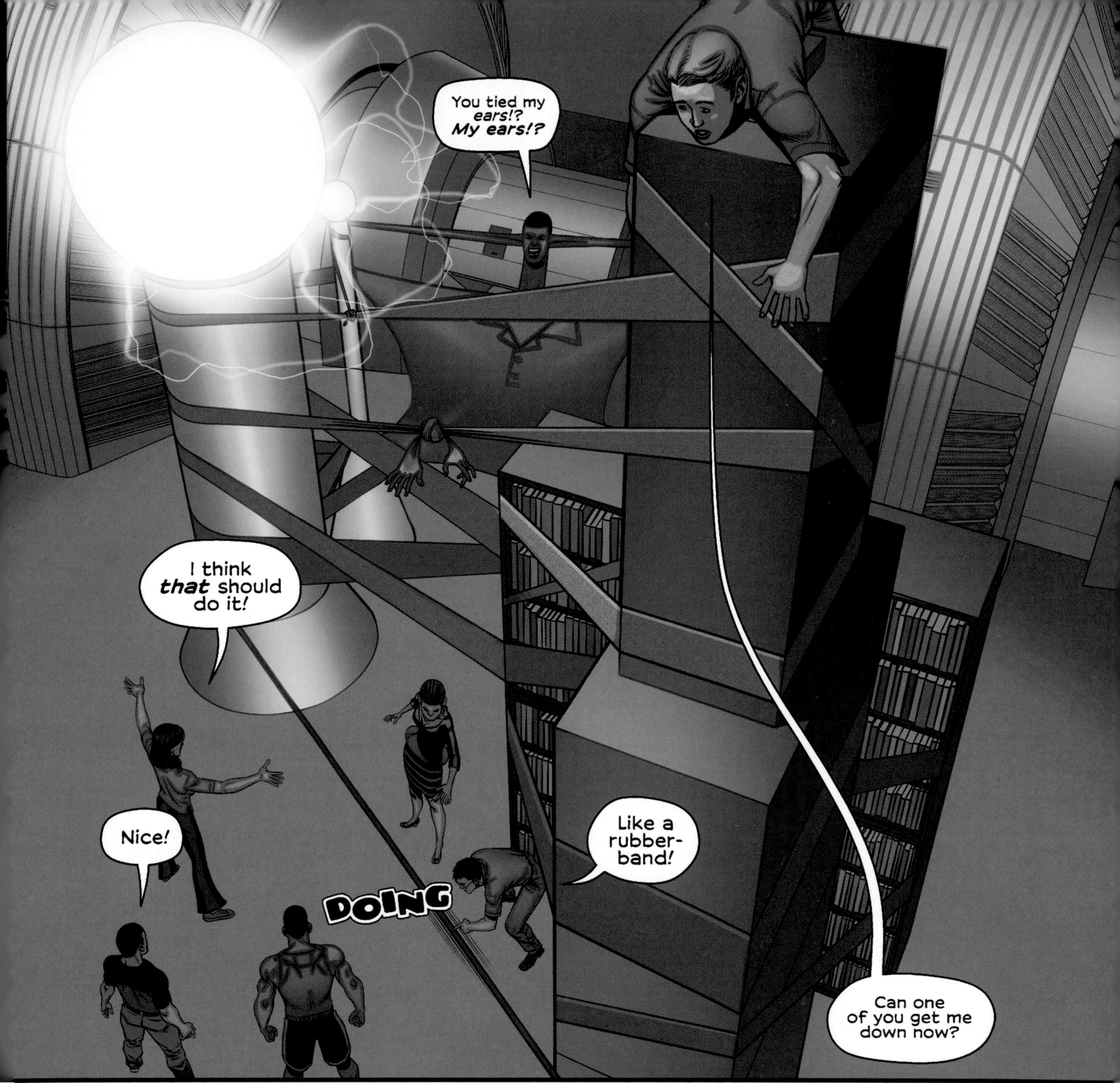
You tied my *ears!?* ***My ears!?***
I think ***that*** should do it!
Nice!
Like a rubber-band!
DOING
Can one of you get me down now?

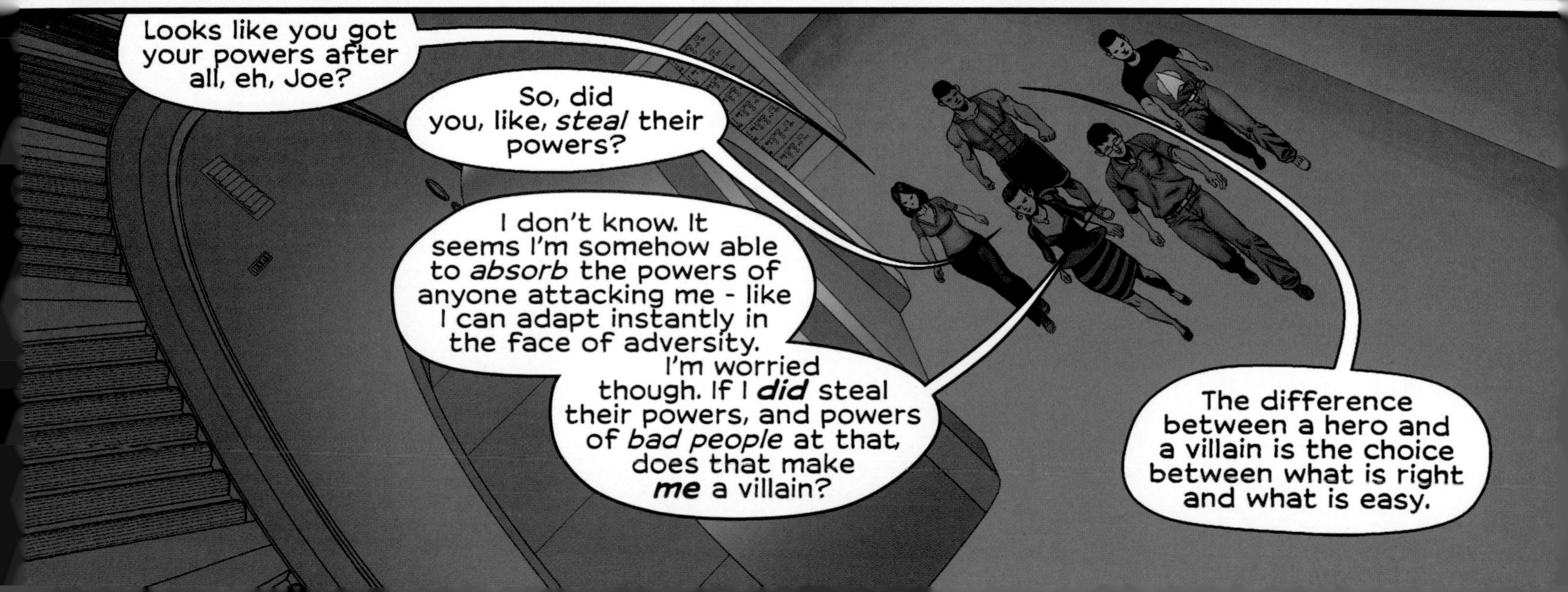
Looks like you got your powers after all, eh, Joe?
So, did you, like, *steal* their powers?
I don't know. It seems I'm somehow able to *absorb* the powers of anyone attacking me - like I can adapt instantly in the face of adversity.
I'm worried though. If I ***did*** steal their powers, and powers of *bad people* at that, does that make ***me*** a villain?
The difference between a hero and a villain is the choice between what is right and what is easy.

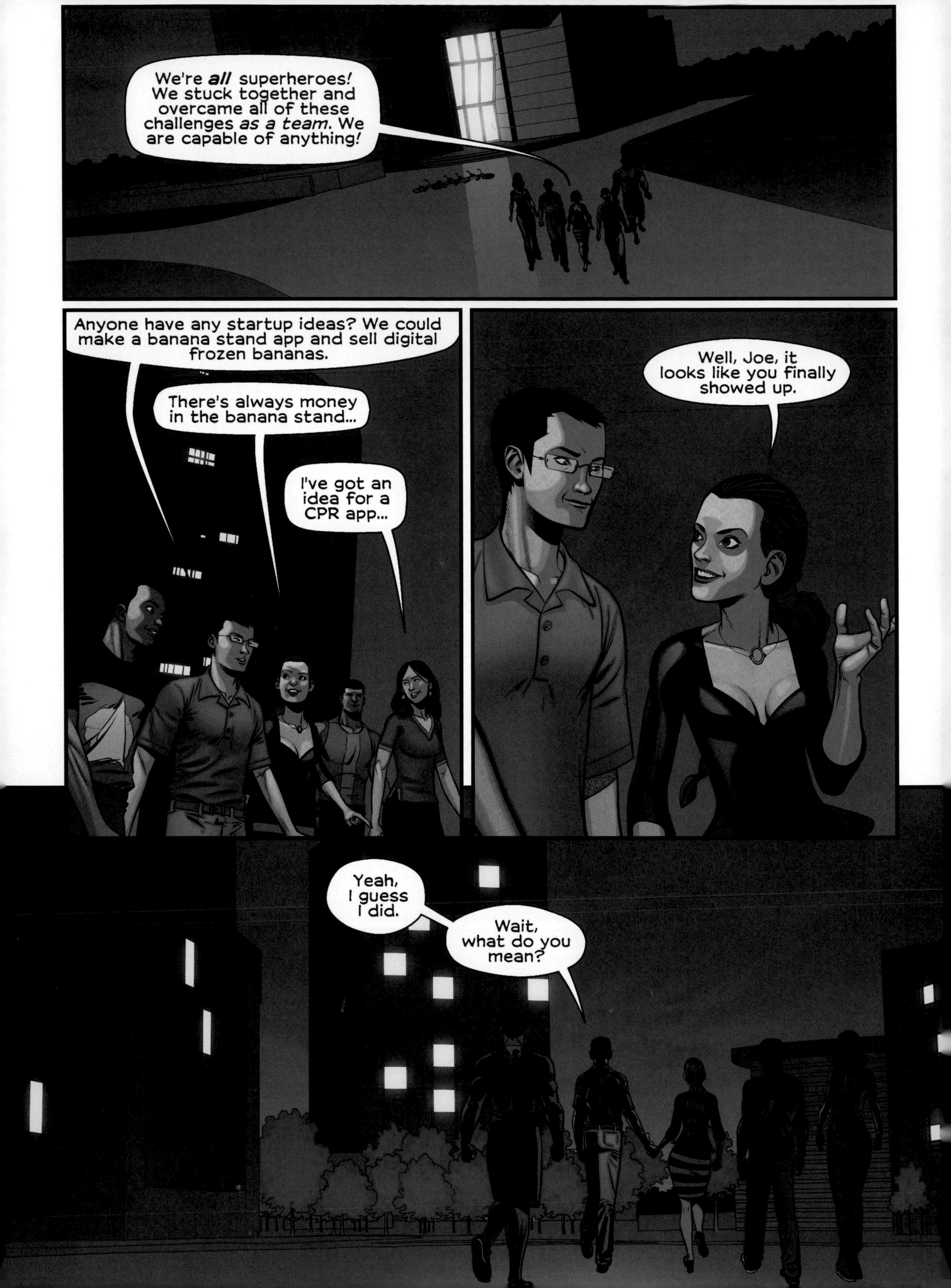
We're *all* superheroes! We stuck together and overcame all of these challenges *as a team*. We are capable of anything!
Anyone have any startup ideas? We could make a banana stand app and sell digital frozen bananas.
There's always money in the banana stand...
I've got an idea for a CPR app...
Well, Joe, it looks like you finally showed up.
Yeah, I guess I did.
Wait, what do you mean?

We all face adversity and challenges in our lives, and we have a choice: Will you simply accept your fate?

Or...

Will you find the courage to put on the cape?

With Great Power...

Afterword by Joseph Floyd

Silicon Heroes started as a research project and turned into an obsession. The story took on a lot of personal details from my life and I hope you will reference the blog on www.siliconheroes.com to read the thought process that went into the nuance and detail of each page.

The main rationale for writing Silicon Heroes was to convey the lessons learned from my career as a venture capitalist. So what are the superpowers of the most successful entrepreneurs? Are entrepreneurs born with these gifts or can anyone develop these character traits?

PASSION

Startups are emotional roller coasters that test the mental fortitude of everyone involved. Every day brings new and unexpected challenges and entrepreneurs can hide under a rock or they can adapt quickly and rise to meet them. Successful entrepreneurs have a fire inside of them that motivates them to push farther and faster than normal. Passion is not just love for your product, team or market. It is the intensity, work ethic and determination that enables sustained effort over a long period of time. Lastly, passion is infectious. Passion can be the glue that brings a group of strangers together and galvanizes them to success on their startup journey.

CHARISMA

Great entrepreneurs achieve amazing results because they are able to maximize the talents and resources of many, many other people. Charisma comes in many forms but ultimately, it is the ability of an entrepreneur to motivate people to align with their vision of the future. Entrepreneurs can use their charisma and leadership to recruit talented people to their team, sell investors to fund their dream and convince customers to bet on their product vision.

SPEED

Speed is one of the only advantages a startup has over a large incumbent. The lean startup framework centers around the mantra of build, measure, learn – build a prototype quickly, measure how users engage, learn from the experiment and then iterate quickly. Cycle time is a critical component for how fast a startup can move through these steps. As a result, in the early days of a startup, the best entrepreneurs set up their company's organizational structure and decision making processes to maximize speed. Another critical aspect of speed is coordination – once a decision is made, an entrepreneur needs to make sure everyone is on board and rowing in the same direction.

FOCUS

Startups are constrained by resources and time. The best entrepreneurs manage these two limited resources through intense prioritization. Founders need to focus the majority of their energy on the most impactful levers that can drive their business forward at any given time. There are simply too many non-essential activities that will take time but not ultimately make a difference. Focus is required to maximize resources in the highest priorities.

FLIGHT

Entrepreneurs are constantly encountering new challenges. The best founders exhibit a type of mental agility that allows them to fly through constant adversity with ease. These founders actively seek out advice from mentors, help from their networks and new ideas from books. These founders have an insatiable appetite for learning and are never defensive when given outside counsel. Furthermore, these successful entrepreneurs are able to synthesize new information quickly and creatively apply it to their business. This mental agility is particularly critical for 1st time entrepreneurs as they are constantly on the verge of ineptitude as their businesses scale quickly. Entrepreneurs who have achieved this level of intellectual agility reach new heights by standing on the shoulders of their network until they can fly.

ACHIEVE YOUR ASPIRATIONS

These entrepreneurial superpowers are skills that anyone can develop regardless of genetics, ethnicity or status. I truly believe that anyone can be an entrepreneur. You don't have to start a tech company – you can coach your kid's soccer team, lead a community food drive or start a new innovation team at work. The real question is: when life blocks your vision of the future, will you succumb to fate? Or, will you find the courage to put on the cape?

"Unless you have a lot of passion, you're not going to survive. You're going to give it up." - Steve Jobs

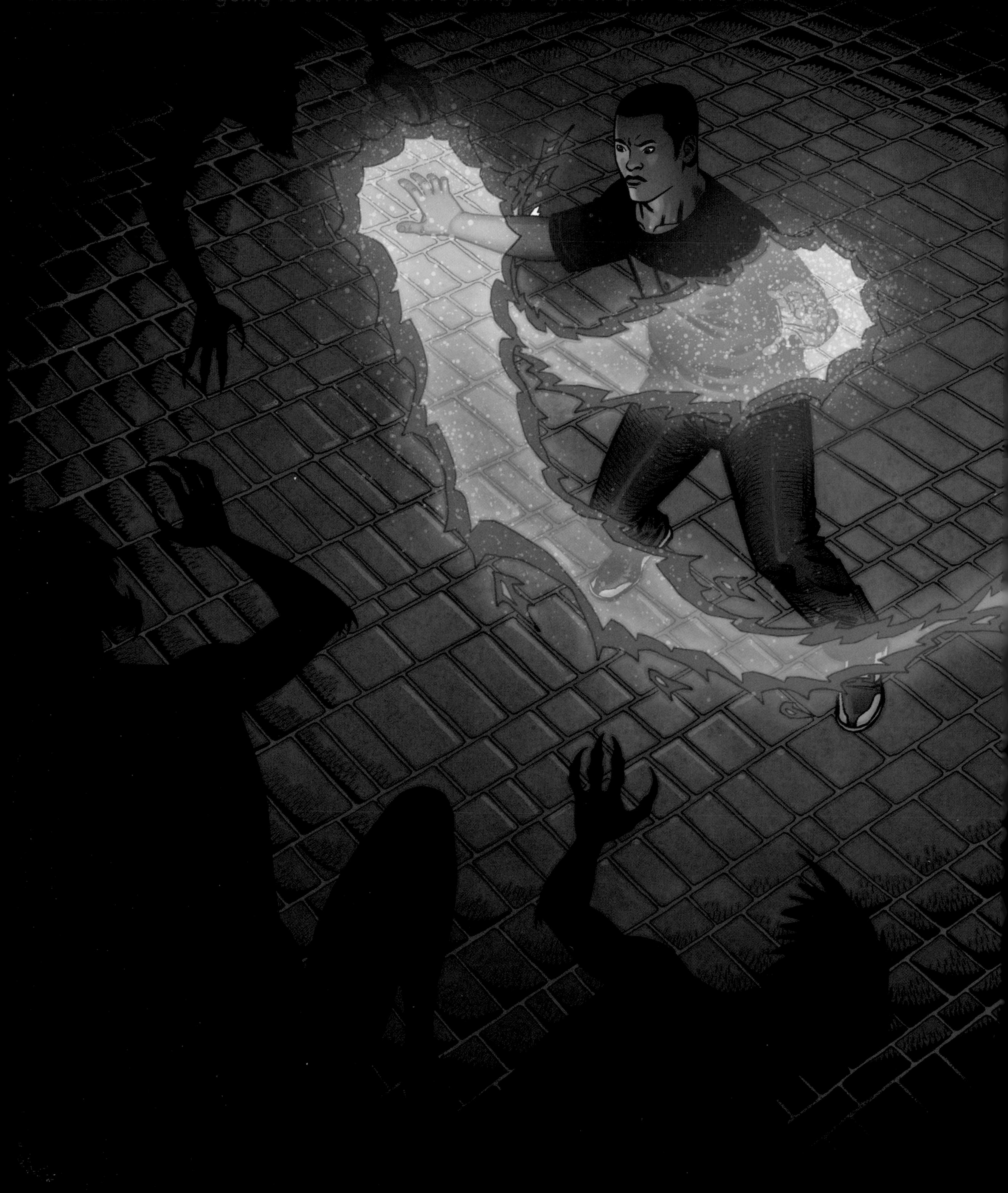

CHARISMA

"Leadership is the ability to inspire others to achieve shared objectives." - Jeff Weiner

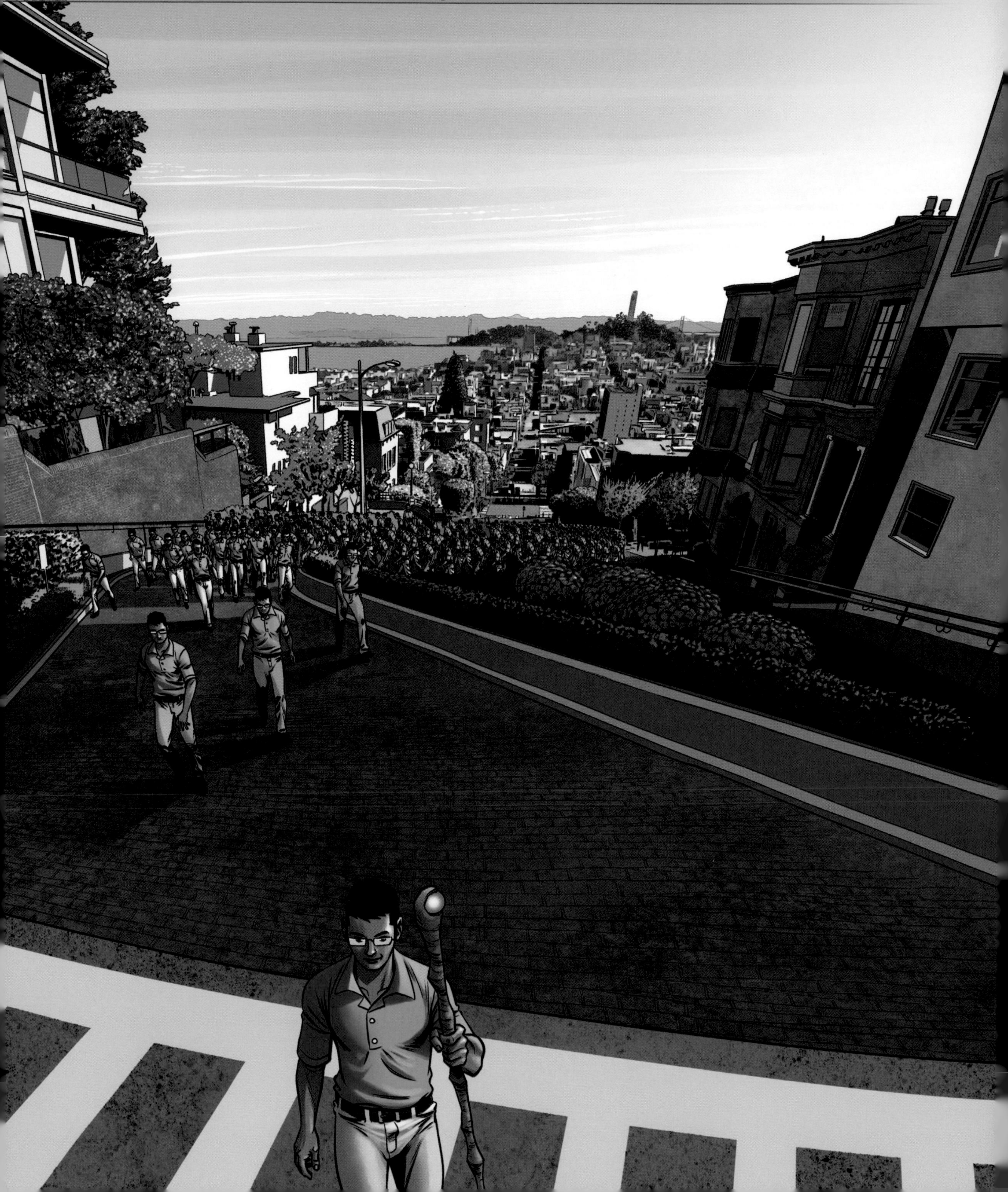

SPEED

"Move fast and break things. Unless you are breaking stuff, you are not moving fast enough." - Mark Zuckerberg

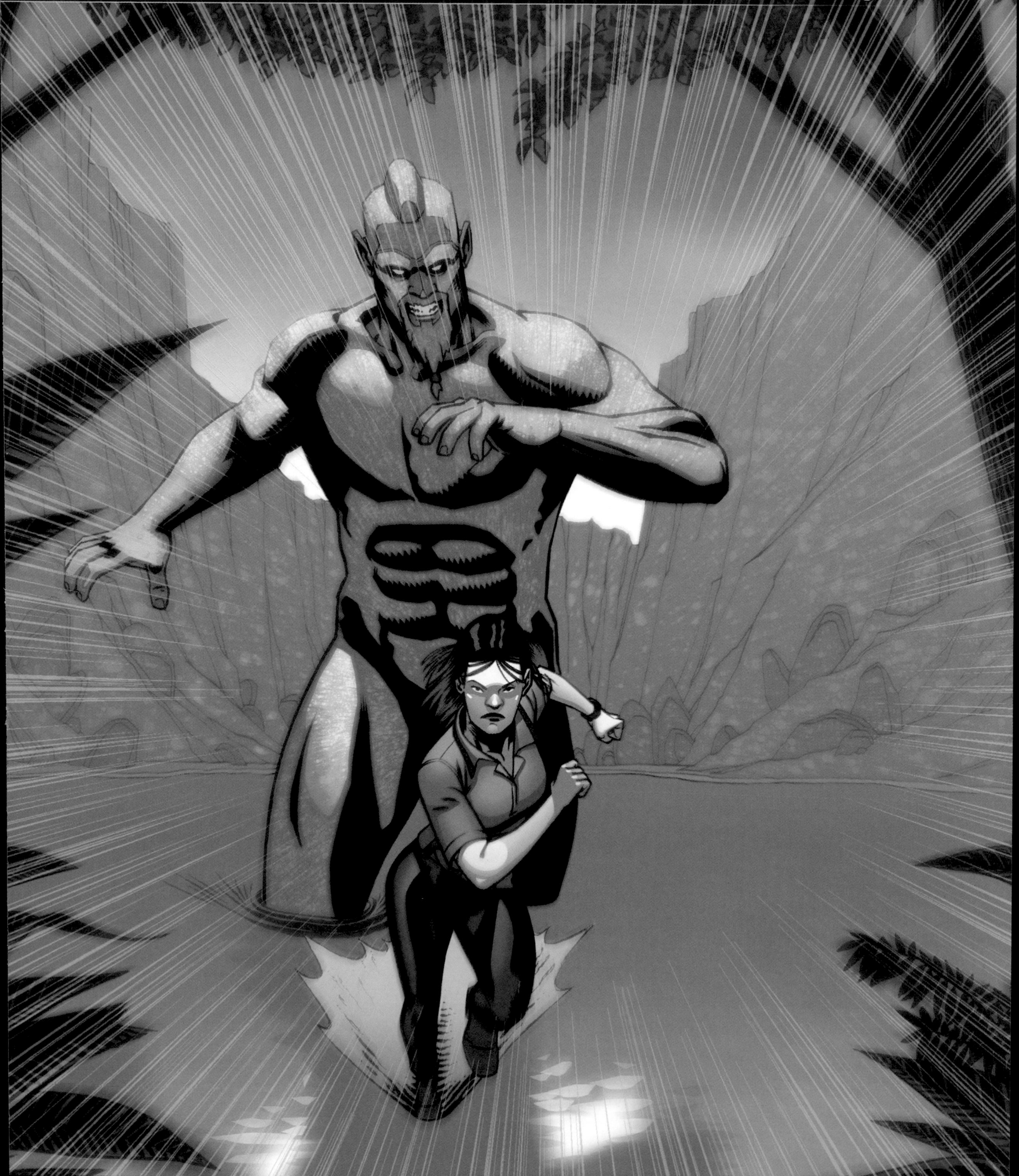

FOCUS

"Focus is key. You can only do so many things well, and you should cast aside everything else." - Tim Cook

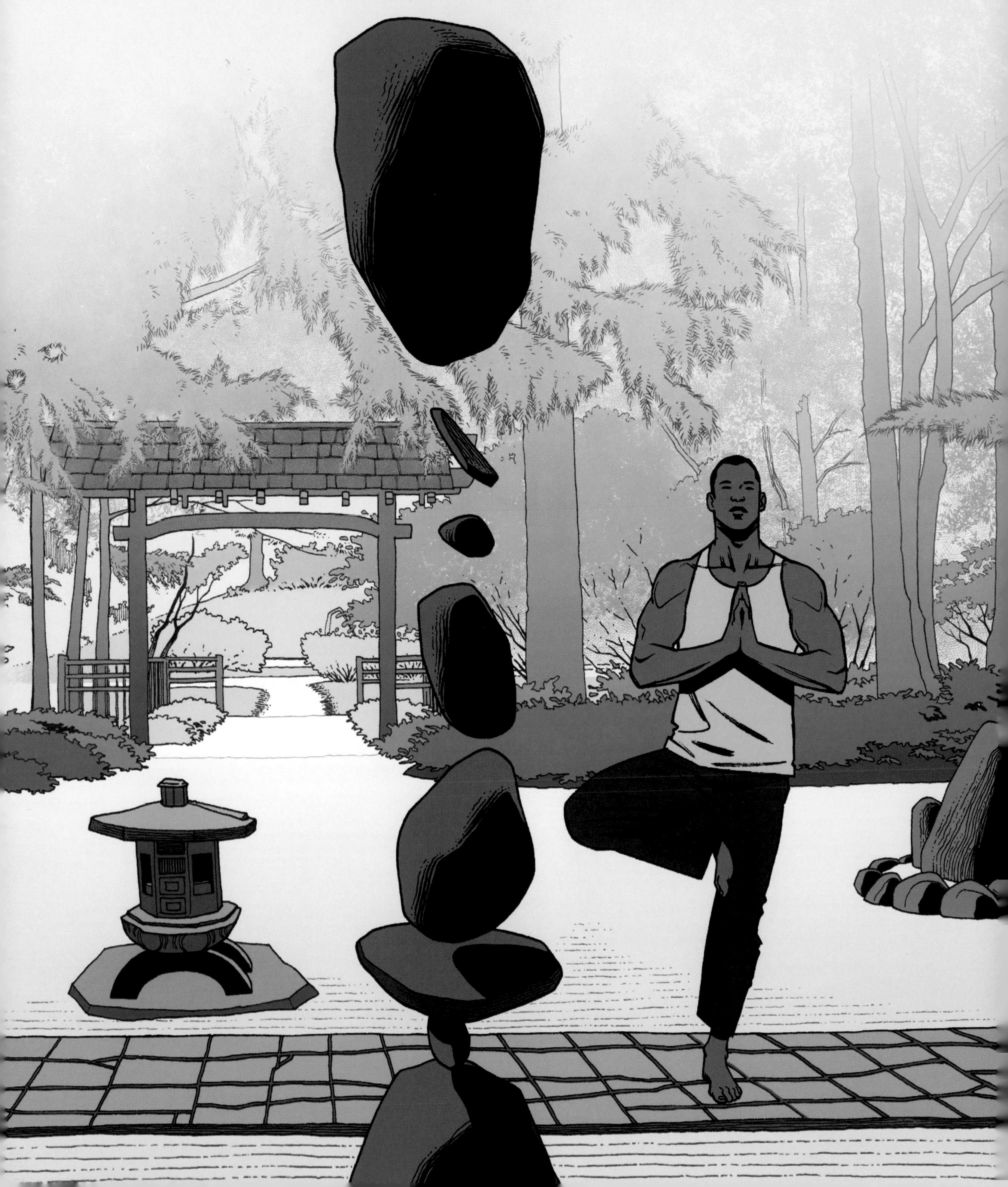

Flight

"Surround youself with people that are only going to lift you higher." - Oprah Winfrey

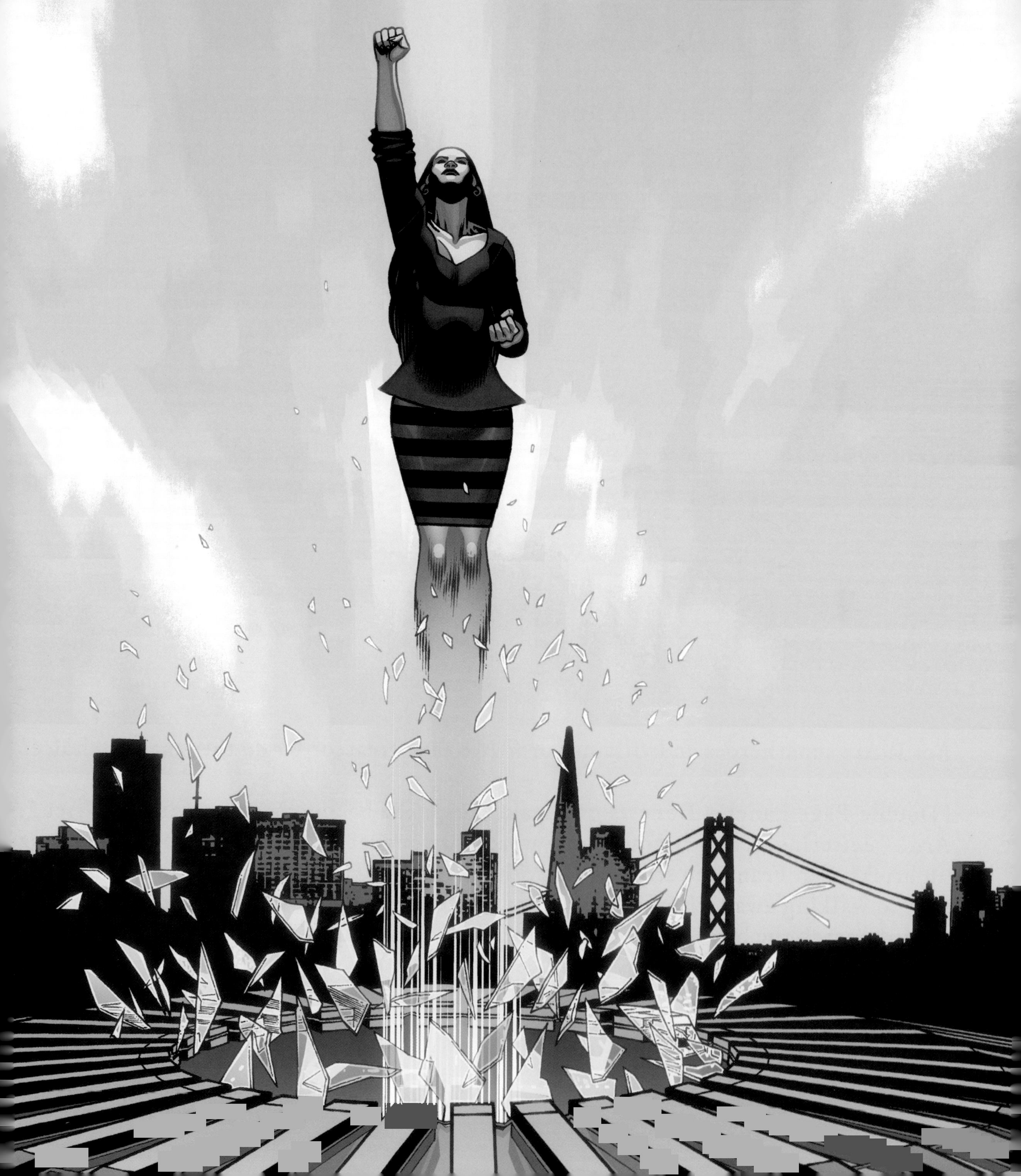

The Origin Story of Silicon Heroes

From Script to Story, Sketches to Illustrations

By Michael Penick

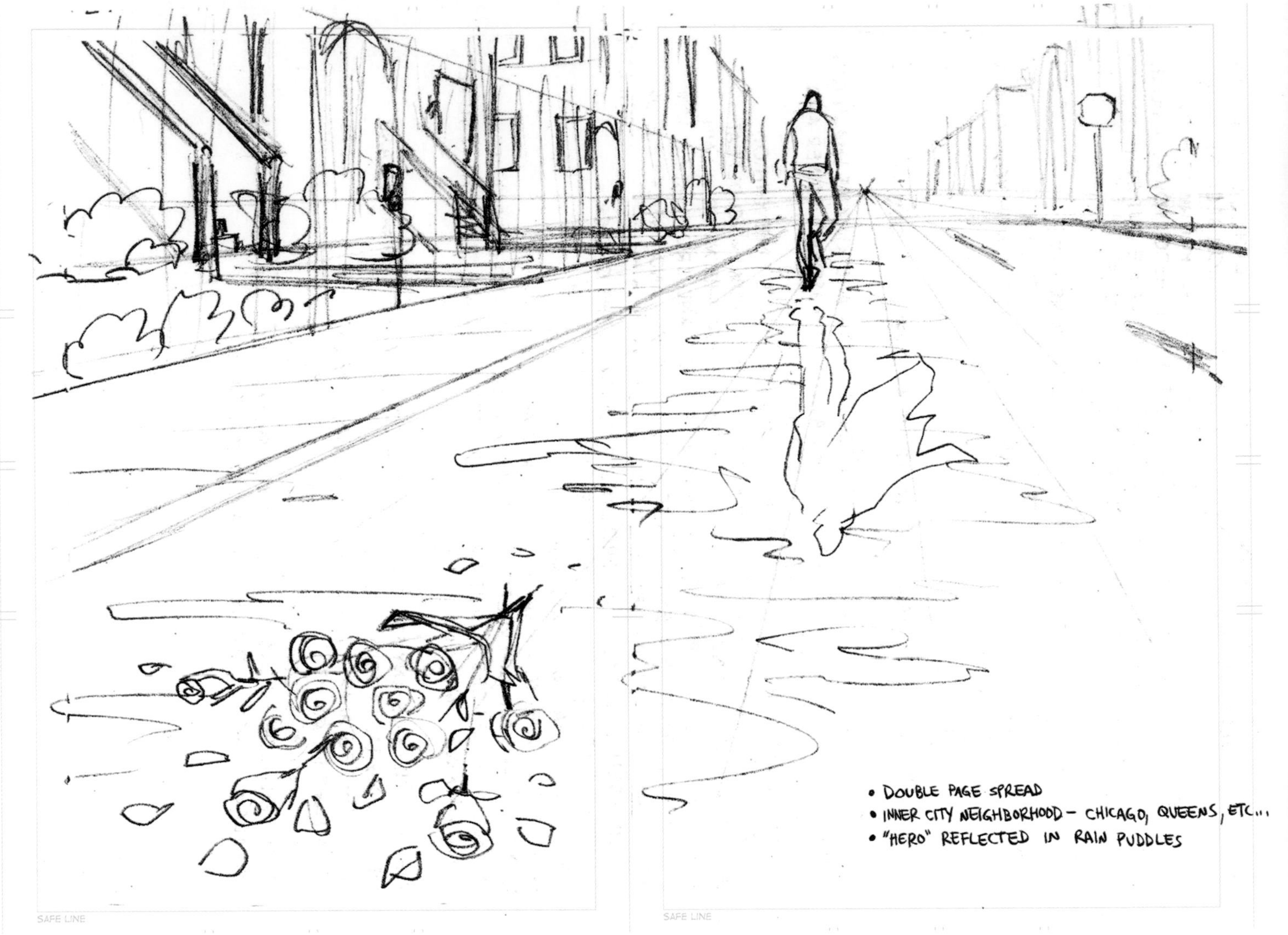

• DOUBLE PAGE SPREAD
• INNER CITY NEIGHBORHOOD – CHICAGO, QUEENS, ETC...
• "HERO" REFLECTED IN RAIN PUDDLES
SAFE LINE
SAFE LINE

Act I: Are superheroes and villains born? Are they created? Or do they make a choice?

[Double Page Panel – Done as grayscale except the bright red roses with the "Act I: Are..." lettering. Dreary, gray, rainy weather. Bouquet of red roses lying in a puddle on bricks. San Francisco street lined with Victorians. High school boy in a disheveled tuxedo walking away with his head down. Streetlamp casts a shadow on the street that doesn't match the boy – shadow of a superhero with a cape. The reader should feel the pain of rejection and love lost.]

Setting The Stage

The opening double page spread is my favorite illustration in the book. When I visualized the original concept, I was imagining the teaser for The Phantom Menace where a young, innocent Anakin casts a shadow of Darth Vader on a wall. I wanted to pull the reader into the story by leaving a number of unanswered questions: Who is this boy? Why is his reflection a superhero? And what are the flowers all about? The illustration is grayscale except the colored flowers to convey the dreaminess of a memory in a style similar to the brilliant backstory flashbacks of Spike from Cowboy Bebop. The original script (lower left) was pretty open ended and Michael really captured the essence perfectly and in painstaking detail.

— Joe

Finding Perspective

I start with a quick sketch on paper (left) to capture the essence of the scene. I then move to digital (below) where I start with the basics: perspective. I usually have a few reference pictures as well, but have to change them a lot to make it work for the composition and story.

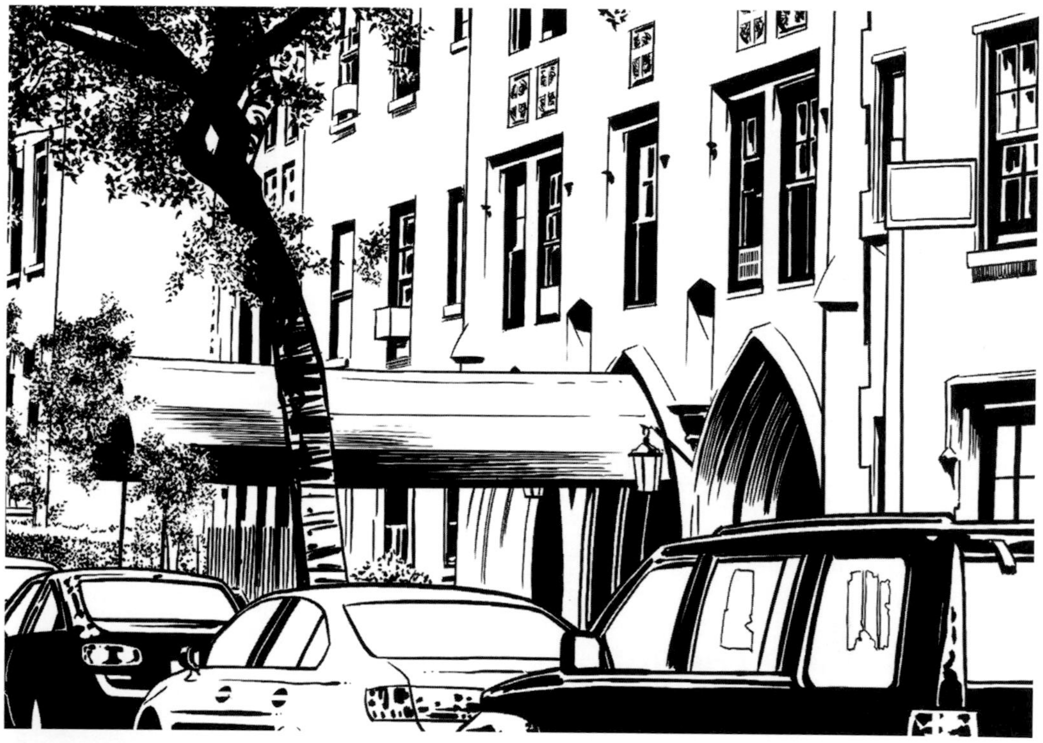

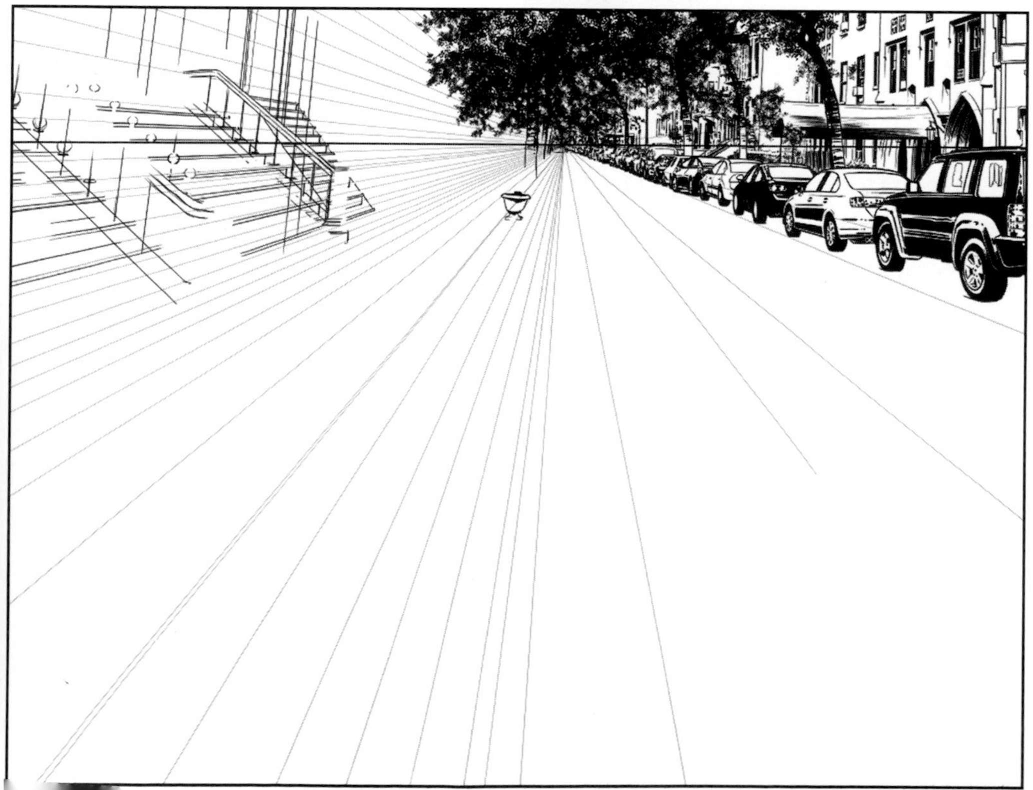

It's All In The Details

This page took me close to a week because of the detail (above). I like the buildings to have character and individuality - those things can make a place truly feel like a real place, or authentic to the location it's supposed to represent, which is important to help the reader get into the story.

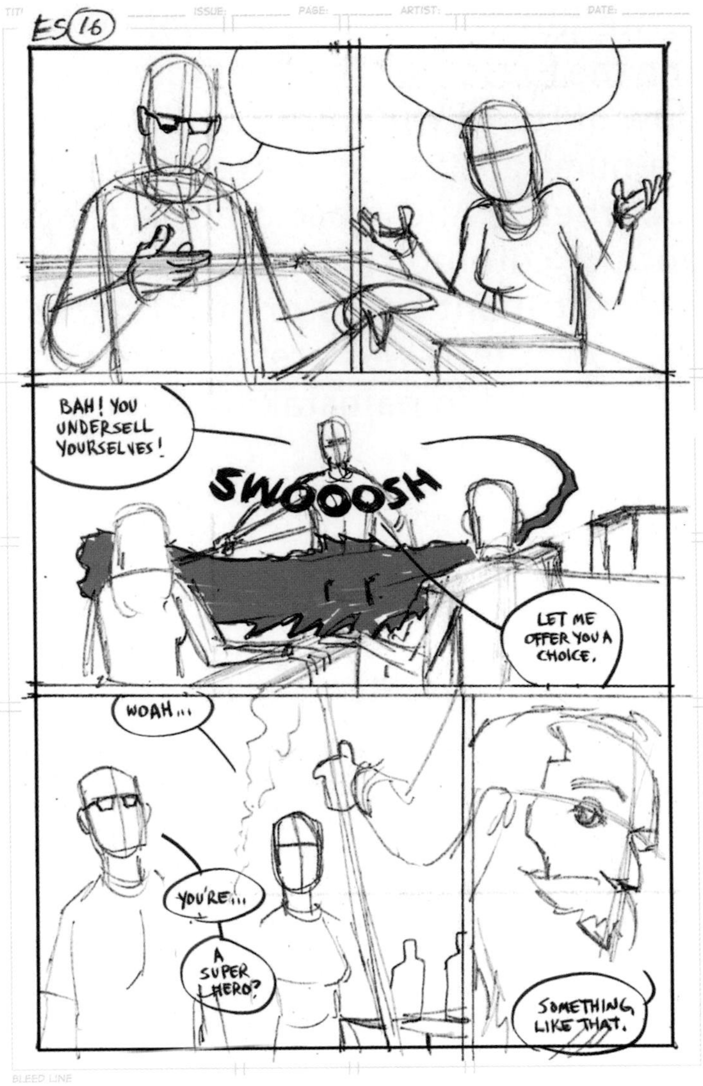
ES 16
BAH! YOU UNDERSELL YOURSELVES!
SWOOOSH
LET ME OFFER YOU A CHOICE.
WOAH...
YOU'RE...
A SUPER HERO?
SOMETHING LIKE THAT.

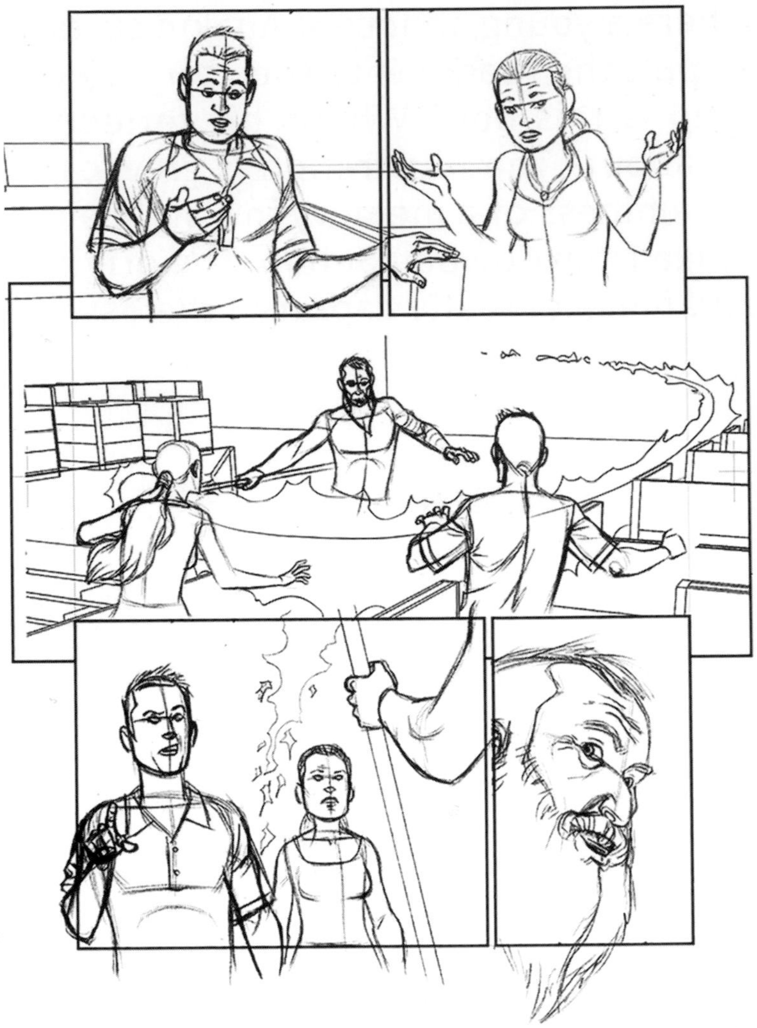

Step 1: The Layout

This is where the words of the script begin to take on a visual life. From the beginning I plan where the dialogue will go so it integrates naturally into the visual flow of the story. Planning the layout in this way ensures that important pieces of art don't get obscured by the dialogue when it's added later on.

Step 2: Pencils

I should put "pencils" in quotations, because I do all the "pencils" digitally - it's so much easier to edit the drawing and make small fixes on the computer than on paper. You'll notice I changed the panel borders in the middle tier to draw more emphasis to the action in that panel. You'll also notice that I always draw the figure underneath the clothes; this helps to ensure I get the folds on the cloth accurate. I also draw beyond panel borders so that stuff stays accurate right up to the point where it disappears off panel.

Step 3: Inks!
Sometimes I do the final line art digitally, using Clip Studio Paint, and sometimes I print them on paper and ink them the old fashioned way - just depends on my mood, really.

The bottom two panels show Mark jumping in as an editor to inject a key foreshadowing sequence. The original script jumps straight to the "choice" where the hero adopts the quest. Mark puts in the little line "Something like that" to foreshadow that maybe the janitor isn't really a hero after all.

Step 4: Colors!
Although I love to color my own work, sometimes there just isn't time. John Rauch, a rising superstar in the comic book business, colored most of this book. John colors it all in Photoshop, using colors to help delineate different scenes from one another, enhance the mood of any given scene, and also ensure that the flashback scenes look appropriately different.

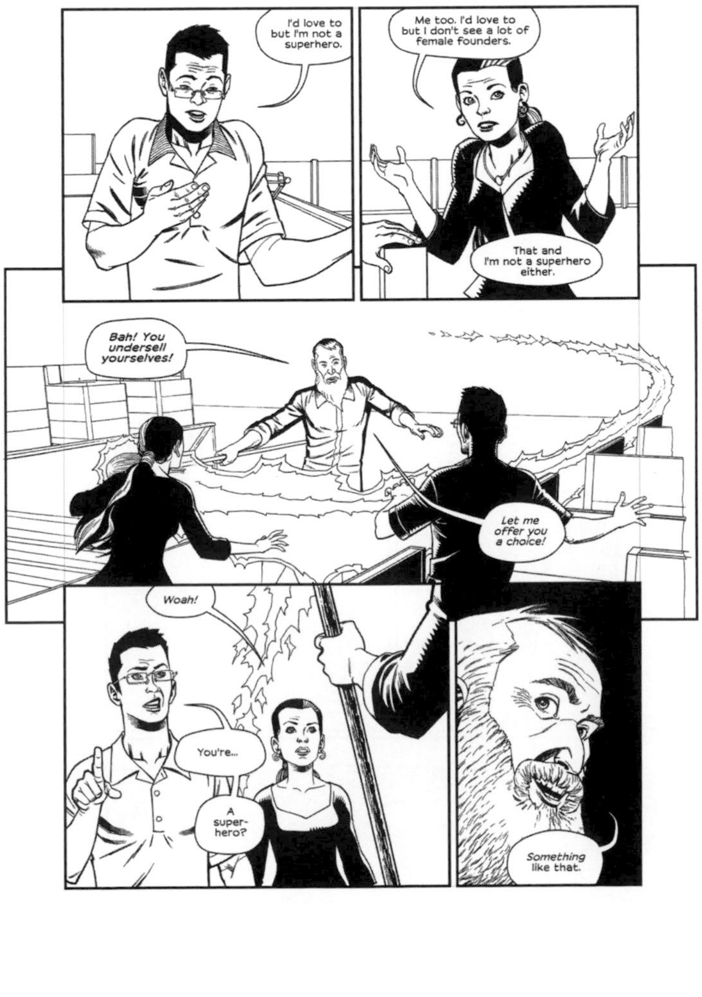
I'd love to but I'm not a superhero.
Me too. I'd love to but I don't see a lot of female founders.
That and I'm not a superhero either.
Bah! You undersell yourselves!
Let me offer you a choice!
Woah!
You're...
A super-hero?
Something like that.

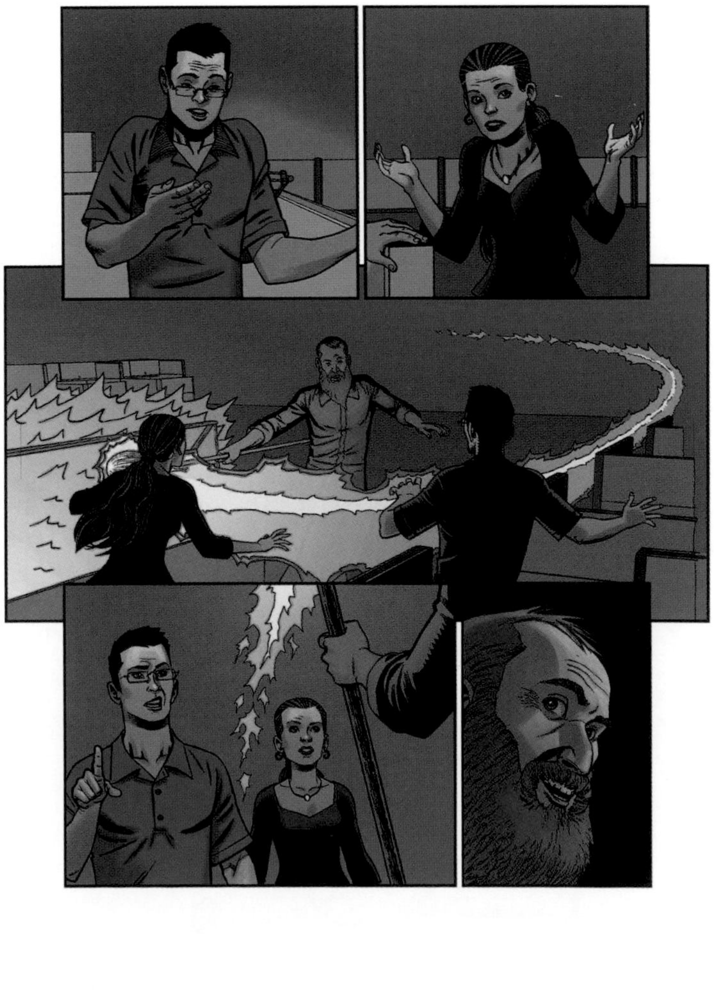

The Backstory of Each Silicon Hero

An Allegory of the Startup Ecosystem

By Joseph Floyd

[Shaun and his superhero gang walks by]
Shaun: Hey loser (to Joe), who is your friend?

[focus on Alexis holding jar with flame]
Alexis: I'm Alexis, I'm new this year and I'm going to win the business plan competition

[Shaun touches the jar uses his ice power to freeze the jar and extinguish the flame]
Shaun: Yeah, right! You're just a girl with a little flame. You could never challenge any of us with real superpowers.

[Shaun walking away]
Shaun: Why don't you stick to being pretty and leave the superhero thing to us. *friends snickering in background*

[back to present - Alexis walking away]
Alexis: Hey, you coming or what!
Joe: *running*

ES 23
I'M ALEXIS, I'M NEW THIS YEAR, AND I'M GOING TO KICK YOUR BUTT IN THE BIZ PLAN COMPETITION.
OH YEAH?
YOU COULD NEVER CHALLENGE US, GIRL
SCHIIIP
WHY DON'T YOU STICK TO BEING CUTE & LEAVE THE SUPERHERO THING TO US.

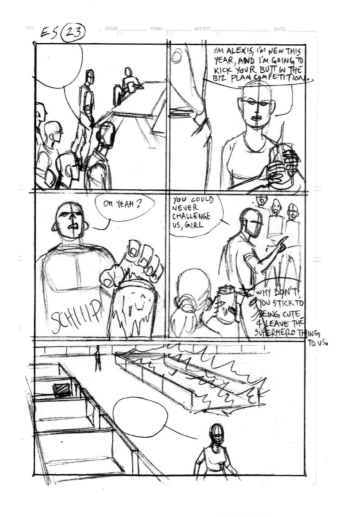

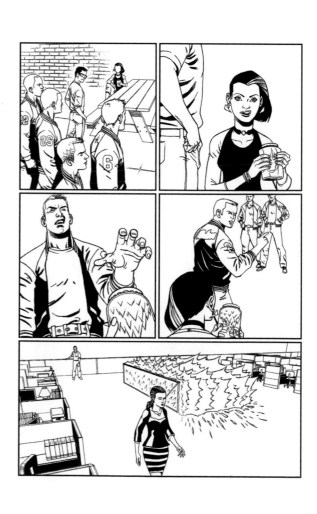

Joe

Joe is the hero who represents the internal struggles of every entrepreneur. He has to overcome aspects of his own humanity, like self-doubt, fear and envy, that impede his ability to succeed. Joe's physical attributes in the story art also counter that of a traditional heroic figure. He is drawn with a small, angular jaw, his shoulders slouch and his head is often looking down. He is often shown from the side or back to show he is not in a position of authority. Joe proved to have the will and the passion to overcome his own internal pressures to emerge a true hero. Unlikely heroes emerge everyday in Silicon Valley, because like Joe, they have made a choice to conquer their fears and redefine what it means to be a hero.

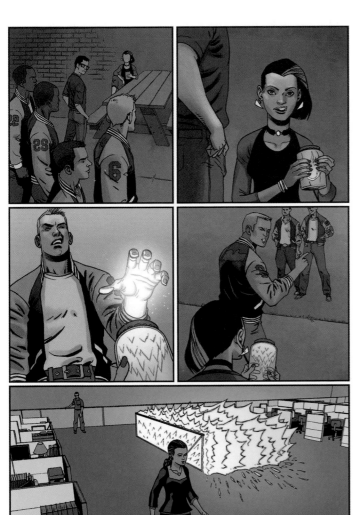

Alexis

Alexis is the hero in the story who fights the external forces that many entrepreneurs must resist everyday. She is self-confident, passionate and visionary but she feels weighed down by the gravity of uncontrollable forces. Her persona is atypical for a woman in business. She is a non-conformist with an edgy exterior and purple hair. Like a startup competing with well established incumbents, she also finds herself up against stiff competition (wearing letterman jackets). With the odds against her, she proves she has the audacity to challenge the norms and break through the inertia of the status quo. She may not have the inherent advantages that would help her coast into the "right" crowd, but she learns how to surround herself with the people she needs to lift her up so she can fly.

Shaun

Shaun is the villain who embodies many characteristics that plague established enterprises like nepotism, entitlement and laziness; qualities that are challenged by Silicon Valley entrepreneurs everyday. To extend the metaphor, Shaun is drawn to look familiar and trustworthy like a classic hero with a strong square jaw and a muscular build. He is positioned in many panels in hero poses where the reader is looking up at an imposing figure (third panel). Much like established organizations that have helped create trusted axioms of industry, Shaun reveals his true nature over time proving that sometimes the widely accepted standards should and can be disrupted.

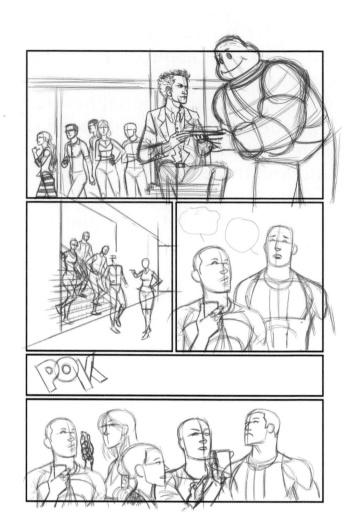

[image of a young man sitting on a swing that is shaking]
(noise: thump thump thump)
Alexis: What's that?

[image resembling a man made of white circular rubber]
Kenny: Oh, that's just the Michelin star chef...
Jackie: ...yeah, everything he cooks tastes like rubber.

[voice coming from next room over through open door]
Alexis: (offscreen) Mail room is down here!

[walking down stairs, into a hallway, room fills with a misty fog]
Jackie: Brrr...*shakes*
Jayne: I have a bad feeling about this.

[loud noise, power shuts off so the background is black and iphones
light people's faces]
Alexis: Shaun must have frozen all of the lights!
Joe: Shaun!!! (yells like Captain Kirk from Wrath of Khan)

Kenny and Jackie

Kenny and Jackie are lovable and indispensable sidekicks. Like R2-D2 and C-3PO, they provide a bit of comedy while simultaneously challenging the reader to question the common stereotypes of an engineer.

Jayne

Jayne represents the gentle giant archetype which every superhero team has to have! Like all of the main characters, Jayne is also a departure from a stereotype as no one would expect the hulking Jayne to love Star Wars so much that he only speaks using lines from the movies. Of course, much like the shocking profundity of Silent Bob, at the end of the story, Jayne is the one that breaks character to deliver his profound insight into the true nature of heroes versus villains.

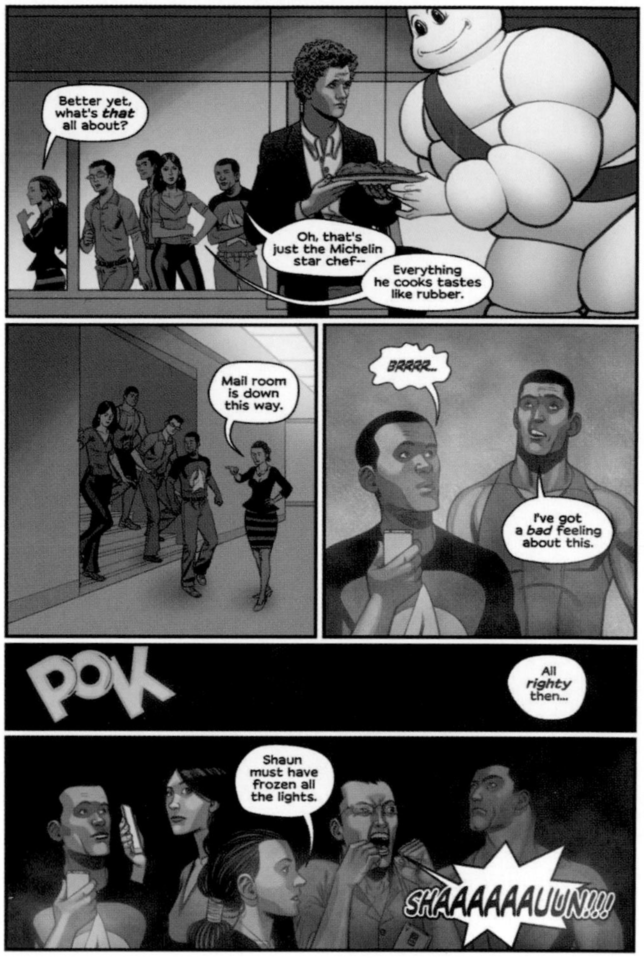
Better yet, what's *that* all about?
Oh, that's just the Michelin star chef--
Everything he cooks tastes like rubber.
Mail room is down this way.
BRRRR...
I've got a *bad* feeling about this.
POK
All *righty* then...
Shaun must have frozen all the lights.
SHAAAAAAUUN!!!

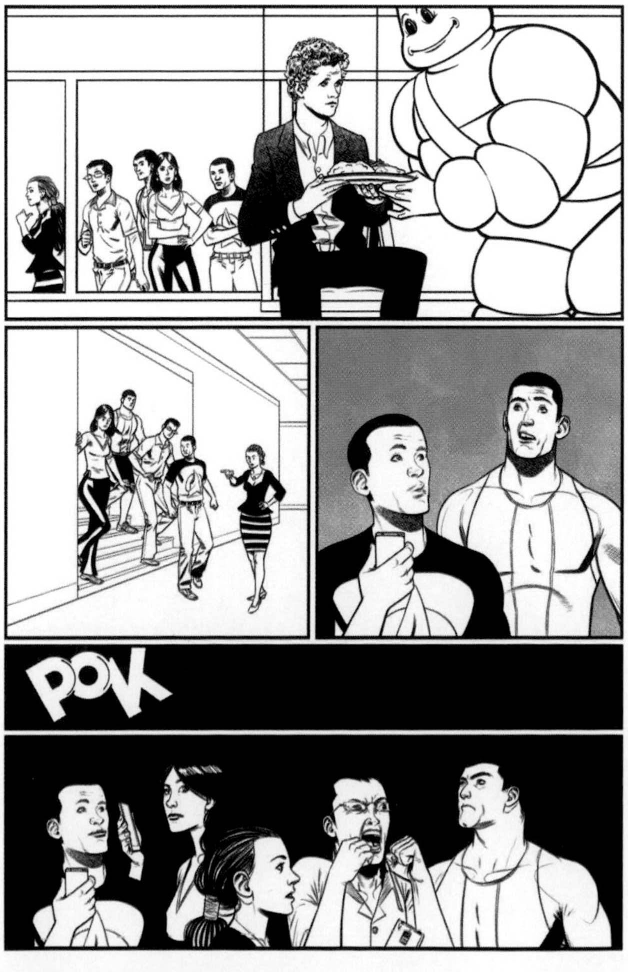
POK

The Farce is With Us

Sigh, I admit it. There are a number of panels in the book that exist purely to set up certain jokes and this page has a couple. The top panel pokes fun at the fact that startups flush with funding will try to recruit employees with ridiculous perks like having a Michelin Star chef cook meals. #thestruggleisreal

The bottom panel is a hat tip to Wrath of Khan and the ridiculous scene where Captain Kirk yells his enemy's name. Yes, I named the villain Shaun just to set up this one small joke...and yes, it was totally worth it.

The Real Heroes

Silicon Heroes started as an online crowdfunding campaign. The response from the community was very generous as we raised over $45,000 from more than 300 contributors. Thank you to all of the Silicon Heroes supporters who helped turn a dream into a reality. Special thanks to the following heroes whose financial support went above and beyond:

Michael Chang
George and Carolyn Cox
Emergence Capital
Ronald and Bessie Floyd
Arlan Hamilton
Malena Iansiti
Gordon and Amy Ritter
Kevin and Christy Spain
SoftTech VC

The vision for Silicon Heroes has always been to promote entrepreneurship and support future generations of entrepreneurs. My wife Alexis is the inspiration for this book, and I cannot thank her enough. To show her my love and support, all profit from the Silicon Heroes crowdfunding campaign was donated to two amazing non-profit organizations: Girls Who Code and Code.org.

Girls Who Code is a non-profit organization dedicated to closing the gender gap in technology. Girls Who Code organizes after school and summer programs to inspire young women to pursue technical degrees and careers in technology. Girls Who Code classes have over 10,000 enrolled students as of December 2015.

Code.org is a non-profit dedicated to expanding school participation in computer science and increasing participation of women and underrepresented students of color. Their vision is that every student in every school should have the opportunity to learn computer science. Since 2013, over 300,000 teachers have signed up to teach Code.org's introductory class and 12 million students have enrolled.

Joseph Floyd

Joe is a Partner at Emergence Capital, a Silicon Valley venture capital firm. Prior to Emergence, Joe did hard time in tech investment banking, private equity and at McKinsey & Co. He is also a proud Cal Bear, a Wharton alumnus and a Kauffman Fellow.

Joe and his wife Alexis live in San Francisco, and they can be found snowboarding in Tahoe, bouldering locally and eating Zachary's pizza.

Favorite Superhero: "My Mom and Dad. They sacrificed and worked tirelessly so that my brother, sister and I could have every opportunity to achieve our dreams. Thank you Mom. Thank you Dad."

Michael Penick

Michael is the most highly regarded artist on the planet Zurtag, which is, unfortunately, not Earth. Back on our little blue orb, meanwhile, he still manages to draw stuff for a living, working for such clients as Sports Illustrated, National Geographic Kids, Marvel Comics, Boom Studios, and many corporate clients you've never heard of. You can see his work, hire him, or ask him to dance like a monkey in a circus at www.penickart.com.

His wife and daughter get to watch him dance like a monkey in a circus every night around the dinner table. It's not pretty.

Favorite Superhero: "Hellboy. Because he's Hellboy. Or maybe detective Christian Walker, aka Diamond (POWERS). Or maybe Iron Man; he fascinated me as a kid. Or Daredevil. Sorry, but picking just one is hard!"

Mark Irwin

Mark has worked with Marvel, DC, Heavy Metal, and many others over the course of his 25-plus year career. Now he oversees Insight Comics, a division of Insight Editions, a fine book publisher.

Favorite Superhero: "A three way tie between my wife and two daughters."